S0-CMP-767

# MEMOIRS
# OF AN
# OUTLAW

## *Life in the Sandbox*

Dear Dad,

Thanks for being there for me
when I was in the sandbox.
I love you,
Pete

## ROBERT M. TANNER III

Neither the United States Marine Corps nor any other component of
the Department of Defense has approved, endorsed, or authorized
this product.

Copyright © 2012 Robert M. Tanner III
All rights reserved.
ISBN: 1477406395
ISBN-13: 978-1477406397
LCCN: 2013900678
CreateSpace Independent Publishing Platform
North Charleston, SC

# DEDICATION

Dedicated to my fellow Outlaws who fought and died in combat and for those who came home but could never leave the fight.

Rest in peace brothers.

# OUTLAW CADENCE

*Got a Detroit Diesel, can you hear my motor hum?*
*Got run flat tires and a bushmaster gun.*
*Got two scout hatches and a coax too.*
*I'm a light armored recon, who the heck are you?*

*Chain Gun, mortar tube, tow on a wire,*
*Speed and mobility, communicate and fire.*
*Screen line, checkpoint, PT run,*
*Captain calls it work but I call it fun.*

*Low right left,*
*Low right left,*
*Low right left right,*
*Outlaws on a run.*

Written by 1ˢᵗSgt. Michael E. Sprague
Delta Company Outlaws, 2004

# CHAPTER 1
# THE BOOK

"Company! Atten-hut!" a gruff voice yelled.

Simultaneously, nearly one hundred and fifty boot heels clicked together, making a very distinct noise in the silence. A door at the back end of a brick building opened, and out walked a tall, weathered-looking Marine wearing a green digital camouflage uniform with his sleeves rolled up. He was clutching a small book in his hand.

He walked with stern determination to the formation of Marines in front of him. When he was about five feet away, the company gunnery sergeant swiftly raised his right arm and saluted.

"Sir, all Marines present or accounted for," the company gunnery sergeant said.

Returning the salute, the company commander thanked the gunny and ended the salute by bringing his arm back down to his side.

"At ease, Marines!" the company commander, Captain Quinlan, said.

Instinctively, the whole company relaxed a bit. Captain Quinlan had us all gather around him in a circle and began to give his usual talk about staying safe over the weekend and telling us not to do anything stupid. As he spoke, my mind began to wander off as I looked around. So many new faces surrounded me, some that I had become familiar over the last few months and some that I was just beginning to recognize. Each man wore the same green digital camouflage uniform, ironed to perfection with no wrinkles to be seen.

The sun was just starting to get to its midday position, and the familiar North Carolina heat and humidity was beginning to take its toll on me. Sweat began to roll down my forehead. Fortunately, on this particular day, the heat wasn't bothering me as much as it usually did. Unlike the others, I had on a pair of shorts and a T-shirt. I stuck out like a sore thumb, but I didn't mind one bit. In fact, it felt good to be different.

Captain Quinlan came to the end of his weekend safety brief and then turned to me.

"Marines, today we say farewell to one of our brothers, Corporal Tanner," Captain Quinlan said with a hint of sadness in his voice.

He called me forward and had me stand next to him. This was the part I had been dreading. I hated being the center of attention, and I really hated giving speeches. Captain Quinlan went on to talk about my history with the Outlaws and the accomplishments I successfully achieved while a member of the unit. I stood in place next to him with my hands clasped together at my waist, nervously twirling my thumbs while I tried to come up with a decent speech in my head.

Captain Quinlan came to the end of his speech, turned toward me, and asked if I wanted to say anything. Here it goes, I thought. The Marines around me began to chant "Speech!" as they waited for me to open my mouth.

"Thank you, sir," I said in a slightly hushed voice. Great way to start it off, Bob, I thought. Nothing like starting my farewell speech sounding like a pansy. After a few seconds, my confidence grew, and I found my voice.

"Some of you I fought alongside of in Fallujah, and some are brand-new to the company. But to all, it's an honor to have served with you." I scanned the Marines gathered around me trying to look for familiar faces in the crowd. I spotted one or two Marines but was slightly disheartened that I didn't see more. So many friends had left the Outlaws once we got back from Iraq, and it hurt watching them leave, knowing I would be one of the few original members left.

"The Outlaws have a proud history, one that has been forged by the blood, sweat, and tears of many fine Marines. Y'all have a lot ahead of you, but I know that you'll continue to proudly represent the Outlaws. I wish everyone the best of luck, and hopefully I'll see you all again some time soon." Short and sweet. I had more I wanted to say, but the words kept escaping me so I kept it brief.

"Tanner," Captain Quinlan said as he came back to my side, "while I wasn't your commanding officer when you were out in Fallujah, it was still a pleasure having you under my command these last few months. As a token of my appreciation, I want to give you this little gift."

He handed me the book that he had been holding the whole time. "This is a book of military short stories. I'm hoping that one day you will write a chapter that proudly represents the Delta Company Outlaws."

I took the book from him and then firmly shook his hand. "Thank you, sir."

"Good luck, Tanner, on all your future endeavors. Semper Fi, Marine," Captain Quinlan said with a sense of finality. He turned to address the rest of the company. "Outlaws, bid farewell to Corporal Tanner, and then you're dismissed for the weekend. Be safe, and have a good one." With that, Captain Quinlan turned and left to go back to the company office.

"Atten-hut!" the company gunny announced. We all stood at attention one more time as the captain walked away.

Once Captain Quinlan had left, the company relaxed, and everyone began to go his own way. Some of the guys I had served with overseas came up to wish me farewell. A few minutes passed, and I was finally all alone, staring at the moving truck in the parking lot with all my belongings in it. I started walking toward it, and my mind began racing all over the place. So this is it, I thought, this is how it will all end. Four years have come and gone so fast, yet I had

had the opportunity to experience so much, things that most people will never get to experience.

I opened the driver's door and slowly sat down in the seat. I turned the key, and the engine came to life. The glare of the sun was beaming through the windshield, so I pulled down the visor. The heat inside the truck was stifling, and I began to make a move for the air conditioner but stopped myself just short of the knob. This is my last day as an active-duty Marine, I thought. Fuck it, I'm rolling down the window and enjoying the wind blowing through my nonexistent hair and taking in the smell of the fresh air.

As I drove toward the main gate of Camp Lejeune with the windows open and music blaring, a flood of memories came back to me. Four friggin' years. I was overjoyed that I was finally able to take on a new adventure, but I was saddened that I was leaving so much history behind. I had made so many good friends. Too many good friends were lost. I was leaving behind a family that I had come to love and had shared so much with over the years. How did it all begin? How did I get to this point in my life and get to experience everything that made me the man I am today? How did I become an Outlaw? And that was when all the memories came rushing back.

# CHAPTER 2
# BURNING TOWERS

My freshly shaven head was resting on my crossed arms as I sat on a chair behind a desk in the middle of an empty room. I'm so friggin' tired, I thought as I sat there trying to catch a few minutes of sleep. What the hell have I gotten myself into? I probably should have thought this through a bit more before deciding to sign the dotted line. Oh well, time for a new adventure in life.

Just a few hours ago, I had been riding on a bus in the middle of the night. We crossed over a bridge and passed through a gate with a sign off to the side that read "Welcome to Parris Island." Our bus pulled up to a stop in front of a brightly lit building just after midnight. Just outside the bus were hundreds of yellow footprints painted on the ground. The door to the bus opened. Here we go, I thought. I had seen it a hundred times in the movies and heard about this very moment from friends and family. Out of nowhere, a tall, muscular Marine dressed in a crisp tan shirt and green trousers stepped onto the bus. The minute he opened his mouth, he did nothing but scream at us at the top of his lungs. It was utter chaos as we all tried to follow his instructions and carry them out as fast as possible. As time went on and night turned to day, more drill instructors came out to yell at us and drive us mad.

Shortly after they gave us what they called breakfast, a frozen Jimmy Dean meal, we were taken to a receiving area where we had to fill out paperwork. The drill instructors had ordered us to sit at desks that reminded me of those we used back in high school. Once we were all seated, backs straight and eyes forward, they told us we were to put our heads down and lie there until our name was called. Since my last name started with a *T*, I lay there for what seemed like an eternity. The only thing that kept me sane was a television mounted on the wall blaring in the background. It gave me a sense of normalcy in all the chaos.

I must have had my head down for at least an hour before I heard a commotion coming from the television. I dared to look up, trying not to let the drill instructors see me. On the screen I saw a very familiar skyscraper with smoke spewing from its side. One of the drill instructors began to turn his head in my direction, so I quickly put my head back in my arms. Why did that tower look so familiar? I thought. And then it hit me. Having lived in the New York metropolitan area for most of my life, I had been to the top of that tower numerous times. It was one of the Twin Towers. But why the hell was it on fire? Before I could think of it further, my name was called. I stood up and made my way into another room to fill out some paperwork.

As I was filling out some documents, I noticed that a lot of the active-duty Marines in the administrative office I was in were talking hurriedly but in hushed voices. I didn't think much of it because I figured they were probably talking like that so we couldn't hear anything.

After I answered a few questions that another Marine was asking me, I was taken into another room where the recruits were being held. None of us spoke, not because we didn't want to talk but more out of fear of having the drill instructors come in and put us through hell again. Thirty minutes passed, and a drill instructor finally entered the room.

"Recruits, get your asses up and make your way through the hatch to my right. Once you get into the room, stand at attention until I tell you to do otherwise!" yelled the drill instructor. We slowly began to rise to our feet, but apparently it wasn't fast enough.

"Oh, you want to play games. OK, good to go. Sit back down!" yelled the drill instructor, his Smokey the Bear hat bobbing as he yelled at us. We began to sit on the ground.

"OK, stand back up!" he yelled. I wasn't even halfway into the sitting position, so I stopped myself and began standing up. We stood up and sat down about fifteen or twenty more times until the drill instructor figured we got the point.

When we entered the room, we all stood at attention. However, the room was small, and with over two hundred men in the group, standing at attention without getting in the way of another guy was difficult. A few moments later, a short, stocky drill instructor entered and told us to sit down. We all immediately dropped into an Indian-style sitting position. There was no way were going to go slow this time around.

The drill instructor moved to the front of the room so we could all see him. His eyes scanned the room as he began to speak. "Recruits," he said in the familiar, raspy drill instructor voice, "a terrible tragedy has befallen our beloved country." Surprisingly, he wasn't yelling at us as we had become accustomed to.

"At approximately zero eight forty-six this morning, a plane was hijacked and flown into one of the World Trade Center towers. Approximately a half hour later, another plane was hijacked and crashed into the other tower." My jaw dropped, as did many others. What the fuck is happening? I thought. It had to be some sort of joke the drill instructors were playing on us. And suddenly it hit me. I remembered the image of the tower burning on the television.

"Recruits, our country has been attacked by terrorists. They have invaded our soil and brought death upon our citizens. This is what you all signed up for. When you complete boot camp, you will be United States Marines. A Marines' sole purpose is to train for war and destroy the enemy. As you go through training, take this shit seriously because you all are going to be downrange fighting these fucking terrorists. Do you understand me?" he said, still with a calm voice.

"Sir, yes sir!" we yelled in unison.

"No, I said, do you understand me?" This time he raised his voice, which was an indication that we had better yell even louder.

"Sir, yes sir!" we yelled, this time much louder.

"Very well, carry on." As he left the room, the other drill instructors who had been standing off to the side began yelling in unison, making us stand up and sit down over and over again before finally leading us out of the room.

That night, my mind couldn't stop going. A month prior to leaving for boot camp, my recruiter asked me what I wanted to do for a job in the Marine Corps. I had scored very high on the ASVAB, a standardized military test, so I was able to pick anything I wanted. I scanned through the list of jobs, and one particular job really piqued my interest: crypto linguist. The recruiter told me that a spot wasn't currently available. I had two choices: I could either wait until the following year when a guaranteed spot opened, or I could go with an open contract and hope for the best. I didn't really want to wait another year, so I asked his opinion about my chances of being a crypto linguist if I went in with an open contract. He assured me that since I had scored so high, I was very likely to get it. I should have known better. Recruiters only tell you want you want to hear. So now what happens, I asked myself as I lay there in bed. So many scenarios played out in my head before my mind shut down and I fell asleep.

*****

A week later, we were finally introduced to our permanent drill instructors, who would be putting us through hell for the remaining twelve weeks. After yelling and playing mind-fuck games with us for a few hours, they took us into our senior drill instructor's room to go over administrative details.

When my name was called, I ran to the drill instructor's office and stood just outside the door with my left shoulder to the wall. About shoulder level there was a yellow handprint painted on the wall. Any time we wanted to talk to any of the drill instructors who were in the office, we had to stand outside of the door at attention, slam our hand as hard as possible against the yellow handprint, and announce ourselves.

I slammed the handprint three times. "Sir, Recruit Tanner requests permission to speak with the senior drill instructor, sir!" I yelled, referring to myself in the third person because we were not allowed to refer to ourselves any other way.

"Get in here, Tanner!" the senior drill instructor yelled.

I quickly entered the room and stood at attention on top of the yellow footprints that were in front of his desk. My senior drill instructor was a short, muscular guy with a permanent scowl on his face. He looked as if he had been to hell and back and beaten the crap out of anyone in his path.

"Tanner, I'm going through your file, and it says you went to college. Is that right?" he said, this time not yelling.

"Sir, yes sir!" I responded.

"How many years did you go to college?"

"Sir, three years, sir!"

"And why the hell did you leave college? You couldn't hack it?" he said mockingly.

"Sir, no sir!" I yelled, frustrated because I knew he was trying to incite me.

"So you couldn't hack it then?"

"Sir, Recruit Tanner could hack it. Recruit Tanner just wanted a new adventure, sir!" I said.

"Oh, so you think this is some sort of vacation, Tanner?" His voice was starting to rise and there seemed to be a hint of anger.

"Sir, no sir! Recruit Tanner just wanted to do something other than go to school, sir!" I was trying my best to explain myself without pissing him off more.

"Good to go, Tanner. Since you're a college boy, you're gonna be my scribe. You understand me?" he said, calming down a bit.

"Sir, yes sir!"

"It looks like you signed an open contract, Tanner. You know what that means, right?" he said with a grin slowly creeping across his face.

"Sir, no sir!" I responded.

"Tanner, it means that you're a dumbass. Some friggin' recruiter took you for a sucker. What did the recruiter tell you that your MOS was going to be?" he asked.

"Sir, the recruiter told me I had a chance at being a crypto linguist, sir!" I responded, concern starting to creep into my voice.

"Tanner, you really are stupid, aren't you? Maybe I shouldn't make you my scribe. Your recruiter is a fuckin' genius. He got you to sign an open contract, and now you're gonna do whatever my beloved Marine Corps wants you to do. In fact, with all that's going on, I'm pretty sure you're gonna be an oh-three-eleven. You're going to the infantry to be a grunt. Your ass is gonna be on the front line, killing the motherfuckers that dared to spill American blood on our turf. That's some good shit, Tanner. I think I'm gonna make your college ass my scribe after all."

"Sir, yes sir!" I said trying to comprehend everything he had just thrown at me.

"You have anything else for me, Tanner?" he asked, sounding as if he was trying to end the conversation.

"Sir, no sir!"

"Then get the fuck out of my office!" he yelled.

"Sir, yes sir!" As was custom in boot camp, I had to request permission to leave. "Sir, Recruit Tanner requesting permission to leave, sir!"

"Tanner, get the fuck out of my office now!"

"Sir, yes sir!" I yelled. I did an about-face and marched out of his room.

I didn't have much time that day to think about the conversation I had with my senior drill instructor. We were too busy getting harassed by the other drill instructors to have time to think. However, once nighttime finally came and the lights were off, I lay in my top bunk bed, and reality began to sink in.

I'm going to be a grunt, I thought. Never saw that happening. But there was no use worrying about it. What was done was done, and all I could do was make the best of it. After a couple minutes, I began to relax a bit and realized that it wasn't so bad after all. One of the reasons I had joined was for some type of adventure, so being an infantryman was sure to bring adventure.

As the night wore on, I began to embrace the fact I was going to be in the infantry. I began to think of all the things that were in store for me. Training, exercises, infantry school, deployments, and the possibility of going to war. War, though, didn't seem like a certainty. We were already being told that we were invading Afghanistan to beat the living shit out of the terrorists who had attacked us. By the time I was done with training, the war would most likely be over, and we'd go back to regular deployments.

Oh well, I thought as I began to close my eyes to get some sleep. Maybe I won't go to war. Hopefully I'll get to do something exciting while I'm in the infantry.

# CHAPTER 3
# FORMATION

A bead of sweat rolled down my forehead. I reached up to wipe it away before it got in my eyes and quickly put my arms behind my back, clasping my hands together at waist level. It was a blistering August mid afternoon, and the sun was at its brightest. What made it worse was that the North Carolina humidity was unbearable, making a relatively modest eighty degrees feel like a hundred. I'm sure the other guys were feeling the heat too.

"Listen up," Gunnery Sergeant Larry Rossignol said in his familiar raspy voice. Standing in front of him were around thirty infantry Marines, including me, in slightly faded camouflage uniforms and polished black boots. "The battalion has decided to expand and add a new company. As the battalion is still out doing training exercises, they've given me orders to begin forming this new company until we get staffed up. A few of you are leaving to go to new commands or getting out of the Marine Corps. Y'all will stay with Charlie Company until you move on. The rest of you will be coming with me to form Delta Company."

There was some slight fidgeting within the formation, but no one said much. Our platoon, part of

Charlie Company, Second Light Armored Reconnaissance Battalion, had been together for more than a year. From predeployment training exercises, which started back in the spring of 2002, to our deployment to Kosovo, Djibouti, United Arab Emirates, and ultimately, the invasion of Iraq, we had become a fairly close group; however, we all knew that eventually the time would come when we would have to part ways.

This was the first platoon that I had been assigned to since entering the fleet after infantry school. Most of these guys were accustomed to moving between platoons and companies, but for me it was a first. My emotions ranged from excitement to sadness. I knew I would be going on a new adventure as part of Delta Company, but I was saddened that I was losing good friends I had made, such as Corporals Jon Hogan, Daniel Nowak, and Andy Wolcott. These men helped me navigate the waters as a new guy and made me a better Marine, passing on knowledge they had acquired over their four years to me. They would soon be leaving to enter the civilian world, and it hurt to see them go. Fortunately, while friends like these were leaving, other guys I had formed bonds with, such as Corporals Jason Sprenger and Jason Klinger, were heading over to Delta Company with me. So it wasn't so bad in the end.

Gunny Rossignol continued on. "The guys that come over with me will form First Platoon. As we bring on more Marines, they will flesh out the rest of the platoon and form the other platoons within the company. We don't have any other senior staff or officers yet, but once the battalion gets back, all that stuff will be sorted out. Does anyone have any questions?"

"When will all this start happening?" someone in the formation asked.

"It's effective starting next Monday. Any other questions?" Gunny asked.

"Where is Delta Company going to be situated?" another Marine asked.

"Across the hall from Charlie Company. Right now it's a mess, so everyone that is going to be part of Delta Company will help clean it up starting Monday. Anyone else got questions?" It seemed as if Gunny was trying to wrap it up so he could dismiss us for the weekend.

When no one said anything, Gunny said, "OK, y'all have a good weekend. Everyone report back here on Monday at zero eight hundred. The guys that are going to Charlie Company will report to me as well until I hand you off to the company. The rest of you will begin helping clean the new office."

He snapped to attention. "Platoon, atten-hut!" he said in a sarcastic tone. Gunny Rossignol had been in the Corps for what seemed an eternity—or how he liked to phrase it to me, "longer than I spent on the ship shitter." He reminded me of Gunny Highway played by Clint Eastwood except with a bit more humor. He'd been an infantryman his whole career, eventually moving on to become a drill instructor and then coming over to Second Light Armored Reconnaissance Battalion to become a platoon sergeant. He'd seen it all and didn't take crap from anyone and absolutely hated some of the formalities, such as dismissing a platoon.

We all snapped to attention. "Dismissed!" he said.

I began walking back to my barracks room when I heard Gunny call me. "Tanner!"

I turned around and saw him waving to me to come back to him. I began heading in his direction at a slow jog.

"Hey Gunny, what's up?"

"You're a college boy, right?" Gunny asked, already knowing the answer.

"Yeah, Gunny."

"And you're pretty good with computers and shit like that, right?" he said.

"Sure. Why, you need me to do something?" I asked.

"Yeah, since it's only gonna be me forming the company for a few days, I'm gonna need some help. I need you to be the company clerk for Delta. You all right with that?" he asked.

Did I have a choice? I thought. "Sure, Gunny, whatever you need." Honestly, he could have asked me to clean shitters all day, and I would have been fine. Over the past year, I had come to have a high amount of respect for Gunny Rossignol. He had gotten me out of a few situations that could have been trouble for me, and he treated us all like men. I looked up to him as a son looks up to his father. I would have taken a bullet for the guy.

"Cool. Once the office gets set up, I'll get you situated and give you an idea of what I need you to do," he said.

"Sounds good, Gunny."

"All right, Tanner. Have a good weekend."

"You too, Gunny." With that, I turned around and made my way back to the barracks. Well, this is going to be something different for sure, I thought. Not exactly what I had in mind going over to Delta Company, but I guess it'll do. I sure hope I like it.

# CHAPTER 4
# CALL SIGN

"Tanner!" called Captain Ladd Shepard.

"Yes, sir," I replied, getting up from behind my desk to make my way to his office.

I stood in the doorway for a couple of seconds while he continued to fill out some paperwork. Captain Shepard had recently been assigned to lead Delta Company as the company commanding officer. Along with Shepard, a few other Marines had come over to flesh out the senior leadership. First Sergeant Michael Sprague, a medium-height, muscular guy had come over from the air wing to take over as the company first sergeant. First Lieutenant Earlie Walker, a short, stern-faced Marine with a thick Southern drawl, was the company executive officer. Gunny Rossignol rounded out the staff and became the company gunnery sergeant. The four of them combined made for quite an interesting work atmosphere—very laid back, something I wasn't accustomed to.

Captain Shepard looked up from his paperwork. "Go down to the ramp and tell the Marines to get in formation on the field," he said.

"Yes, sir." I turned and headed out of the back entrance of the company office. The walk to the "ramp," our slang term for the parking lot and maintenance hangars that were home to our light armored vehicles (LAVs), wasn't very long. In just a few minutes, I was walking past several LAV-25s, huge armored vehicles with eight wheels, a troop bay in the back that held four infantry Marines, and a 25 mm Bushmaster chaingun mounted to a turret on top. They were awesome to look at—unless, of course, you were the enemy; then you'd just shit your pants and run the other way.

I went around to all the platoon sergeants and informed them that they were to get their Marines in formation. The platoon sergeants started calling out to their Marines that they needed to head over to the field. One by one, Marines began to appear from behind, on top of, and under the vehicles where they were either maintaining their equipment or scrubbing off rust from the vehicle.

About a half hour passed before the whole company was formed up on the field. A hundred and fifty-eight Marines were standing in perfect columns at parade rest as Captain Shepard made his way out onto the field. When he reached the front of the formation, First Sergeant Sprague called us to attention and reported in to Captain Shepard.

"At ease, gents!" Captain Shepard said, slowly making his way closer to the formation.

"I've got a couple of things to pass down to you all before you head out for the weekend. First of all, I'm pretty sure many of you are aware we still don't have a company name."

It was true. We still didn't have a company name, and it had been nearly a month or so since we had formed up. All the other companies in the battalion had names, and we stuck out like a sore thumb without one.

"First Sergeant Sprague, Lieutenant Walker, Gunny, and I have been discussing it, and we've got a few names we want to throw at you."

He began to rattle off a list of names like "Renegades" and "Warriors." They were fine but didn't seem to suit us well. As we continued to reject the names one by one, it became obvious that Shepard was getting a bit frustrated.

"How 'bout the Outlaws?" someone yelled out.

The name seemed to roll off the tongue rather well, and I really liked it the moment I heard it. A lot of heads were nodding in approval, so I could tell the other guys liked it too.

"Outlaws," Captain Shepard said, almost as if he were asking a question. "Outlaws," he repeated one more time. It seemed as if he was trying to gauge the masculinity of the word, ensuring it represented us well as a fighting unit.

He looked up and could see a lot of us were quite pleased with the name.

"Y'all like the name?" he asked.

"Ooh-rah!" the company shouted in unison.

"All right, Outlaws it is!" he proudly declared.

"OK, Outlaws, I've got another thing I want to talk to you about," Captain Shepard said, his voice taking on a more serious tone. "You may have heard through the rumor mill that the Outlaws may be assigned a certain mission. Well, I'm here to tell you those rumors are true. We've been given orders to begin training to deploy to Fallujah, Iraq. I'm not certain exactly when we will be deployed, but I know that it will be sometime in the January to February time frame. Over the next few weeks, we're going to be going through a lot of paperwork and conducting various training exercises, so just prepare yourselves and your family."

Hushed whispers could be heard throughout the formation. We had all heard that something like this was coming, but we didn't know how true it was or how far out it would be. The time frame Captain Shepard gave us put the deployment only three months away, which was not typical for a predeployment workup. It meant that we would be busting our asses to get things done as fast as possible to ensure we would be ready to go when given our actual deployment date.

"I'm sure you all have a ton of questions," he continued, "and we'll do our best to answer them when we get more word. For now, go back and begin to mentally prepare yourselves for the deployment. First Sergeant Sprague, inform the Outlaws that they're dismissed for the day."

First Sergeant Sprague snapped to attention and saluted Captain Shepard. "Yes, sir," he said, ending his salute and turning around to face the company.

"Outlaws! Atten-hut!" he shouted, proudly calling out our new name.

In perfect harmony, we all snapped to attention. "Platoon sergeants, dismiss your Marines," he said.

"Yes, First Sergeant," the platoon sergeants said in unison as they saluted. The platoon sergeants turned to their individual platoons and began dismissing them one by one.

I started making my way back to my barracks room. So many things were going through my head. The deployment wasn't really news to me because I had overheard the officers talking about it in the office. Being the company clerk did have its advantages. It still rattled me a bit because the time frame for deployment was coming up quickly.

There was also a part of me that was annoyed I was the company clerk now that we knew we were being deployed. The last thing I wanted to do was waste my skills as an infantryman sitting behind a desk out in the middle of Iraq. I have to figure out something, I thought, or I'll go crazy out there.

My thoughts quickly turned toward the new name. The Outlaws. It had a ring to it, and it certainly represented us well. Over the past couple of months, our company had begun taking on Marines from various companies within the battalion as well as units outside of it. Some of us had worked together in the past, but the majority of us were strangers to one another. We constantly butted heads with one another, and our company as a whole had butted heads with the battalion on more than one occasion. We were the outlaws of the battalion, so the new company name was very fitting.

*****

The next couple of months were a whirlwind of madness. We eventually found out our deployment date was going to be sometime in February of 2004. They couldn't give us a firm date due to security issues. With only three months to prepare, we worked from dawn to dusk getting our vehicles to combat-ready status. All of the platoons trained nonstop for different scenarios and missions. Wills were being written. Personal finances were being sorted out. New equipment was being issued constantly. Personal effects were being sent back home. This was the chaos and turmoil typical of a hasty predeployment.

In January of 2004, I decided to press Captain Shepard and First Sergeant Sprague to allow me to go over to one of the line (infantry) platoons; I didn't want to be the company clerk when I was in Iraq. I wanted to put the knowledge and skills I had learned from my previous deployment to the test. First Lieutenant Knox Nunnally and Second Lieutenant Ronny Rowell knew of my desire to go back to being a scout, and they also pressed the captain. Eventually he gave in but put me in the platoon that I had not wanted to be in initially, First (Red) Platoon. The platoon commander and sergeant were new to the company, and many of the Marines in the platoon complained that they were overachievers and too rigid.

First Lieutenant David Snipes was in need of a scout team leader for one of his vehicles. He tested my knowledge and decided I was fit to be a team leader. I was happy; I might not have been in the platoon I wanted, but I was doing something I was trained for and enjoyed.

Our platoon, along with the rest of the company, trained non-stop to become a well-oiled machine right up until we deployed. A few of us were sent off to different schools to learn new skills that would aid us in our deployment. I, along with seven other Marines and

Sailors from the company, went to an Arabic class, where we learned how to read and speak basic Iraqi Arabic. Additionally, the platoon received various classes introducing us to Arabic culture, urban warfare, improvised explosive device patrols, and other subjects that pertained to our overall mission in Iraq. We needed to learn how to win "the hearts and minds" of the Iraqis.

We deployed to Kuwait on February 28, 2004. We left Kuwait for our new seven-month "vacation" home, Fallujah, Iraq, on March 15, 2004. When we left the United States, we went with 158 Marines. There was a one-in-five chance that a Marine would be seriously wounded, slightly wounded, or killed. Eight of our brethren, our brothers, died during combat missions. Another seventeen were seriously wounded or were sent back due to various medical reasons. The Outlaws returned to Camp Lejeune on September 28, 2004 with 133 Marines.

Throughout my four years in the United States Marine Corps, I witnessed many things, but nothing compared to what I was about to experience over the next seven months.

# CHAPTER 5
# THE FLIGHT

What a horrible flying experience. Whatever could have gone wrong the day we left, happened.

Our company was split into two groups to load onto two military cargo planes, C-130s. Each group was set to leave at a certain time from Camp Lejeune via bus to go to Cherry Point, NC. From there, the group of Marines would load up onto a plane to begin the journey to Iraq.

I was in the second group. This was probably the only good thing that occurred that day. The day we left happened to be payday. Since we were leaving later in the day, I left early in the morning to run down to the PX so I could buy a new Gameboy and some games for the ride and deployment, things that would keep me busy during my down time.

By the time I got back, I found out that the first group had already left. Since I had nothing else to do, I went back to my room to make sure I had everything. I went through my mental checklist of gear and when I was sure I had it all, I lay down on my bare mattress and took a quick nap.

About an hour or so passed when I was awoken by some guys talking outside of my door. I listened to their conversation to see if it was anything important.

"This is fuckin' bullshit," one of the Marines said. "We pack up, head out there, and not twenty minutes go by before they send us back here." He seemed pretty pissed off. "Then we get back and I'm about to drop my pack when they tell us we have to head back out. Halfway there, they turn us around and tell us there's a possibility that all flights will be cancelled. I hate this hurry and wait bullshit." The conversation continued on for a few more minutes before they left.

I could understand the frustration. I would have been just as pissed if I were in his shoes. Everyone was already on edge because we were leaving and this nonsense was just agitating people further. The rumor that all flights would be delayed until the next day wasn't helping, either. When I heard that last bit about all flights possibly being delayed, I became a bit ticked off. I had no phone, all my gear was packed up into my sea bag and carry-on, and I had nowhere to sleep. I sure as hell didn't want to take everything out again just for one night's sleep.

A few hours passed and our group received word that we were going to give it a try. We threw on our gear (rifle, MOLLE pack, and MOLLE harness), grabbed our carry-on bags and sea bags, and loaded onto our bus.

The ride to Cherry Point was about twenty minutes. When we got there, we were guided into a building where we had to wait around some more. This was the military's motto at its best: hurry up and wait. We rushed like hell to get everywhere, and when we got there, we sat around forever.

After about an hour's wait, the company executive officer, First Lieutenant Earlie Walker, had us all get into alphabetical order to be weighed. We all needed to be weighed with our gear on to ensure that the plane did not exceed its maximum carrying limit. I walked up to the scale and watched the scale numbers climb. With all my gear, I weighed 260 pounds. Normally, I was only 180 pounds.

Shortly after I got weighed, the word finally came down that the flight was going to take off as scheduled, so we lined up single file outside of the hangar to board the plane. From the outside, the C-130 looked as if it might provide a decent ride for us, but as the saying goes, never judge a book by its cover.

The pilot and navigator, both Air Force officers, were welcoming us aboard. I was way in the back of the line, so I could only imagine what the inside looked like. I had never been on a C-130 so by the looks of the outside, I was imagining a huge interior with tons of room to stretch out my legs. Boy, was I in for a shock. I stepped onto the plane, turned right, and realized I was in for one hell of a ride.

The plane was split down the middle by a cargo net fence. On the left and right side of the plane were cargo-netting benches attached to the wall. The benches also came out of the cargo-netting fence. Fan-freakin-tastic. Nothing like riding coach.

There were about a hundred Marines in my group. I ended up halfway down the bench on the middle left side of the plane. Since we had very little room, each Marine had to interlock his legs with the Marine to his front. So basically, we all had our legs in each other's crotches. There was no aisle room anywhere.

As if things couldn't get worse, there was a huge temperature variation on the plane. Those toward the rear of the plane near the cargo door and those in the front of the plane near the cabin had no heat at all. It was absolutely freezing. Most of them went into their gear to take out their black bear pullovers or poncho blankets to stay warm. Luckily, everyone was so mashed together that body heat was able to provide some warmth. The middle of the plane was a different story. It was a sauna. This was where I was. Most of us had taken off our camouflage blouses so we could cool off in our t-shirts.

From the outside, we must have looked like a mess. Everyone was jammed together. Rifles were poking into people's legs. Some guys were nodding off on someone else's shoulder. Someone somewhere was snoring. A couple people were eating snacks; others had taken out portable DVD players or video game consoles. Once in a while you could even catch a guy pissing in a bottle because he didn't want to cross a sea of legs to get to the front of the plane. Honestly, we were an absolute mess.

Once the plane took off, I tried to make myself as comfortable as possible given the situation. I stripped down to my t-shirt, pants and boots so I could cool down a bit. Trying my best not to elbow the guys to my left and right in the face, I rummaged through my carry-on to get my Gameboy and one of the games I purchased.

"Whatcha playin'?" a Marine to the right of me asked as I settled down.

"Madden 2004," I responded. "Just picked it up today from the PX."

"Cool," he said, looking over my shoulder trying to get a better view.

"When I'm done, if you're still bored, you can borrow it. I didn't get much sleep last night so I'm just playin' til I pass out," I said.

"Sweet, dude. Thanks."

I played for about thirty more minutes before I could feel the exhaustion start to set in. My eyes were half slits and my head was slowly drooping down. I was about to put the Gameboy away when I remembered the promise I made.

The Marine who I had spoken to earlier was reading a book so I nudged him with my knee.

"You still want to play?" I asked.

"Yeah, if you don't mind," he said as he put down his book.

I handed him the Gameboy and a couple other games and then went about the process of forming my camouflage blouse into a makeshift pillow. It only took a few minutes before I passed out.

Six hours after departing from Cherry Point, we arrived at our first stop, some small airfield in Newfoundland. Everyone thought of it as a weird place to land first. We all believed we were going straight to Ramstein Air Base in Germany.

It was about five in the morning when we landed, and snow covered the whole airfield. We offloaded and rushed inside the building, where we were let loose for an hour to do what we wanted. I went to the small restaurant to have a nice, warm breakfast. Others flocked to the phone centers or small stores, and others just sat around and slept or smoked. Once the hour was up, we were all herded back on board for our next stop, Ramstein Air Base.

We landed in Germany about eight hours and one hell of a backache later. This time we were told we had two hours to goof around, which was more than enough for us to cause a little trouble and feed our faces. This base seemed to be better equipped for a horde of starving Marines. There was a mini mall with a Burger King, a Pizza Hut, and a few other small places to eat. There were also a few shops and a phone center. Some Marines flocked to shops and food stands that had women working there. Somehow they believed that since they wouldn't see a woman again for seven months, they might be able to get a little action before they left or maybe even a number. Typical Marines.

I went with a group of friends to get some chow from Burger King and then headed to a store to buy another game for my Gameboy. Hell, I thought this was the last time I would be able to buy something to entertain me. Eventually we all headed back to the airport facility to wait around for the signal to load back up. Some guys nodded off for a few minutes, and the rest lined up near the phones to get in one last call.

About a half hour later, we got the word to load back up. We all packed in like sardines and went back to sleeping, video games, movies, and reading. No one really knew what was in store for us.

# CHAPTER 6
# KUWAIT

After a long and uncomfortable, ten-hour, knee-to-groin flight, we reached our final destination, Kuwait. I was under the impression that we were going to fly into Kuwait Naval Base, which would have been too good to be true. During my first deployment to Iraq, we had offloaded our ship at the base and staged our assault into Iraq from there. From what I remembered, Kuwait Naval Base was like the Disneyland of the Middle East—good stores, good food, and lots of stuff to do.

But then reality kicked back in, and I remembered I was a Marine. We never got the nice stuff. Instead, we landed at Camp Wolverine to start preparations for our drive to our next staging point. All I remember about Wolverine was that it had a bunch of sand, giant tents, and palettes of water everywhere.

An Army admin service member guided us to one tent and had us drop all of our gear. He then directed us to another tent where we did some paperwork and sat down to await a debrief on our ROEs (rules of engagement) and other rules that we needed to follow in Kuwait and Iraq.

The brief was the typical crap some legal person back in the States usually came up with. It was never realistic. They showed us a few short videos of what we might see in Iraq and how to handle certain situations. Then an Army lawyer came out to answer any questions we might have. Every scenario we came up with, this guy had the answer.

"So, let me get this straight, sir," someone behind me asked, interrupting the lawyer. Everyone's head turned to look at the Marine speaking. "If some haji with an AK is in a crowd of people screaming 'Allah Akbar' or some crap like that, waving his gun in the air and then starts pointing his gun at me, I can't do shit until he fires at me?"

All heads snapped back to look at the lawyer, awaiting his response.

"That's correct," the lawyer replied. I could hear a few "Ain't that some bullshit" and "We're gonna get fuckin' killed" responses murmured in the background.

The lawyer went on to answer a few more questions before he left. Based on what he told us, we were to follow the ROEs to a "T" and not stray. We had to follow the Geneva Convention guidelines or face punishment under the UCMJ (Uniform Code of Military Justice). Obviously, whoever came up with these rules never faced combat situations because I honestly doubt that person would wait until an insurgent pointed a gun and fired directly at him before firing back.

Once the lawyer had left, a group of Army personnel began to hand out small cards with the ROE's and other rules on them. We were told to keep them in our left breast pocket with our military I.D.; that lasted three weeks, about the time it took for the sweat to soak through our cammies and turn our cards into mush.

We found out that we were going to stay the night at Wolverine so people made their way back to our sleeping area, pulled out their magazines, video games, and anything else to occupy the time. I started playing a little football with a few buddies and eventually pulled out my lucky hacky sack and got a group of people together to "hack" a bit. The day passed with no new word so we all piled into our hooches (tents) and called it a night.

The following day brought with it a new leg of the journey. We found out we were moving closer to the border to an Army base called Camp Victory, the place where our LAV's were awaiting us. The only thing we really needed to know about the base were the essentials: a PX, good food, and phones. We loaded back onto the buses and made way for our new temporary home.

After serving four years in the military, I had come to realize that it was full of sarcasm and humor. If Camp Victory was what victory was supposed to look like, I would have hated to see what defeat was. Camp Victory was a huge sandbox with a bunch of tents and a couple of buildings that housed the command center. Our company occupied four tents on the east side of the base, and the parking lot for our vehicles was a square marked out by concertina wire with port-a-johns by the side.

When we got off our buses, Gunny was standing by to pass word on the camp rules, tent setups, company fire watch, and layout of the base. Each platoon was assigned to a hooch. We ended up sharing ours with Weapons Platoon. Everyone grabbed a cot and set up his gear and personal belongings as he saw fit, space permitting. Once that was in order, the next thing on everyone's mind was food—where was it and how did it taste. Gunny informed us of the chow hall locations: the fast-food location with pizza and chicken wings (the good stuff) was a short walk north of our tents; the air-conditioned chow hall with delicious breakfast and cold drinks was a half-mile walk across base. So during the hot days, we would eat fast food, and in the morning we would eat at the chow hall.

Once the vehicles were up and running, we did a few movement exercises to see how they ran. Then, the next step was to see how their weapons fired. About a week before our departure to Fallujah, we left to go outside of Camp Victory to a firing range to test them. The exercise lasted about four days and showed us that nearly half of the weapons were not operational, so we went back to camp and tried all over again. We continued to work on the vehicles to ensure that they were operating correctly. Everyone worked night and day to get them to combat-ready status, especially the mechanics.

And that was pretty much how the rest of the week passed. Each day was about the same as the next. The daily routine was something along the lines of: wake up, shit, shower, shave, eat, go to the PX and phones, fire watch, basic classes, eat, prepare vehicles and restore them to combat ready status, goof around, eat, go to the PX and phones, and, sooner or later, sleep.

March 14, 2004. Gunny Rossignol and Lieutenant Walker took a few Marines and left for our eventual home to prepare it for our arrival in advance. The rest of us packed our belongings and loaded up the vehicles. After doing as much as we could to prepare for our deployment, our company was sent to the staging point, where we were attached to a convoy heading into Iraq. We moved our vehicles into position and hunkered down for the night, imagining what might be in store for us the next day.

# CHAPTER 7
# STAGING POINT

In the distant background, I could hear a CH-47 passing overhead. The rhythmic thump of the blades as they sliced through the air was soothing as I lay half asleep under our makeshift tent.

"AAAAAAAHHHHHHHHH!"

I was suddenly awakened by a commotion. I leaped out of my sleeping bag and saw Lance Corporal Josh Shearer, the saw-gunner for my team, running away from our vehicle, half naked.

"It's landing on us. The helicopter, it's gonna land on us," Josh said repeatedly.

Apparently, Josh was in a deep sleep and had heard the helicopter in the distance. In his dream, he believed that the helicopter was going to land on us, so he was trying to run away from the vehicle to find some kind of cover so it wouldn't land on him. But instead of dreaming it, he actually did it.

"Shearer!" I yelled at him after he had run about fifty feet. "Get your crazy ass back here! It was just a helicopter flying overhead. It's already gone, dude. Just chill out." I was trying my best to calm him down a bit.

Shearer started walking back but still appeared shaken. "I coulda sworn it was gonna land on us Corporal Tanner," he said in his thick Nashville accent.

"You got issues, Shearer," I said, trying my best to hold back a laugh.

"Shearer, get your ass back to sleep before I put you on fire watch," Sergeant Krall mumbled from inside his sleeping bag. It was never a good thing to wake up Krall from a deep sleep.

Shearer made his way to his sleeping bag but couldn't avoid being teased by a few of the others he woke up.

"Y'all can kiss my ass!" Shearer said sarcastically. Once he finally realized the hilarious situation he found himself in, he couldn't help but chuckle. After we all had a few laughs and teased him a bit more, we went back to sleep to rest for the long day ahead of us.

\*\*\*\*\*

"Wake up, Tanner."

Staff Sergeant Randy Phelps was hovering over me with a cigarette dangling from his mouth.

"Get your stuff together and then wake up the rest of the scouts," he said, cigarette smoke pouring out of his nose as he exhaled.

I stretched to get all the kinks out and then slowly squirmed out of my sleeping bag. I stood up and saw that Sergeant Michael Krall, my vehicle commander, was waking up the rest of the vehicle crew. I gently nudged Josh with my foot to wake him up.

"Don't worry, Shearer. There's no helicopter landing on us...this time," I said jokingly.

"Ha ha, very funny," Shearer said before flipping me the bird.

After I was sure Shearer was getting up, I walked around the vehicle to wake the other scouts: Corporal Miguel Forsyth and Lance Corporal Todd Herman.

About a half hour later, the entire convoy was stirring and packing up what little they had taken out to sleep. I ensured that my scouts had packed up their gear and that the scout compartment of the LAV-25 was neat. After the vehicle and my team were situated, we all sat down to eat an MRE (Meal Ready to Eat) while we waited for word to be passed down. As I ate, I glanced around at the rest of the convoy and noticed most of the Marines were doing something to kill the time: hacky sacking, reading, eating, or just chatting away. Eventually, Lieutenant Snipes came back to our platoon's location.

"School circle at Red 2. Lieutenant Snipes is going to pass word," someone yelled from the distance.

Everyone stopped what he was doing and started walking over to Red 2's position. Once we were all gathered and the team leaders and vehicle commanders ensured that their Marines were present, Lieutenant Snipes started to pass word and give us our op (operations) order. In essence, we were told our placement in the convoy, how we were conducting the convoy, and rules of engagement.

In my opinion, our placement made no sense. We were the biggest, most heavily armed and armored vehicles in the convoy, yet they decided to throw us in the middle. To make it even more frustrating, the convoy's assault and security elements consisted of Humvees. The Iraqi terrain is ideal for LAVs. The vehicles can get up to around 70 mph on the flat, open areas, negotiate any obstacle presented, and maneuver more effectively than a Humvee, but most importantly, the LAV can take a lot of small- to medium-arms fire and unload an immense amount of firepower in return. So the idea of our sitting in the middle of the convoy bothered us all to no end.

The next thing that bothered us and continued to haunt us throughout the duration of the deployment was the rules of engagement. We were not to engage the enemy unless the enemy showed intent to fire at us. We were not to fire unless told to do so. We were not allowed to retaliate unless we could positively identify the combatant. To sum it up, we couldn't do a damn thing except get shot at and smile.

Finally, the information that seemed to matter most to us was the future—what were we going to do and how was it going to happen. Lieutenant Snipes informed us that we would travel along MSR (main service route) Tampa for approximately eight hours until we reached our first stopping point, Camp Scania. At that base, we would refuel and temporarily rest for the second part of our journey. When the road march resumed, we would travel from Camp Scania, along MSR Tampa in a northerly direction, until we reached MSR Mobile. Around the intersection of MSR Mobile, we would meet up with a detachment of Army Humvees who would escort us to our final destination: Camp Baharia.

All the team leaders, myself included, and vehicle commanders were busy writing all the instructions down and highlighting the routes on their map boards. When the orders were finished and Lieutenant Snipes felt confident that everyone in the platoon understood the instructions and his duties, he gave the command to mount up.

# CHAPTER 8
# ROAD MARCH

The air resonated with the sound of about a hundred engines starting up. Dust filled the sky as the vehicles started to move about. This is it, I thought. This is what I have been training for. I could only imagine what lay ahead.

I looked down through my hatch into the scout compartment to ensure all my men were good to go. Lance Corporal Shearer was standing up through his hatch taking in the scene. Corporal Forsyth was sitting in my side of the scout compartment with the PRC-119 (man-pack radio with a handset) strapped to his back and the handset in his ear. He kept giving me updates of what was going on over the net. Lance Corporal Herman was on Shearer's side of the compartment with his rifle between his legs.

I stood back up and donned my CVC (communications) helmet to listen in on the net and receive any further word from Sergeant Krall. Lance Corporal John "Ski" Martuszewski, our vehicle gunner, clicked over to the vehicle intercom and started repeating some joke that someone had told over the platoon net. He then went on to tease our driver, Lance Corporal Tyler Tracy.

Tracy sat quiet in his driver's compartment and sweat like a pig. All the guy did was eat, sweat, and sleep. During our whole deployment, I don't believe I ever once saw him not soaked in sweat. However, it was understandable because he sat right next to the engine block, he was completely shut in, and he had no ventilation. But we had to tease him because that was how we showed our friendship for one another.

"Tracy, how you doing down there?" Ski asked.

Tracy, never one to say much, remained silent.

Ski wasn't one to let someone ignore him so he continued. "Tracy, if you don't crack open your driver's hatch, you may drown in your own sweat."

I let out a little chuckle and I could hear Krall do the same. But still, Tracy didn't respond. He was probably cussing Ski under his breath.

"Tracy, what the fuck did you eat man? I can smell that shit from up here! You must be sweatin' whatever you ate out of your pores dude. Damn that shit stinks!" Ski continued, doing his best to get a reaction.

"Ski, you're soooo funny," Tracy sarcastically said. He had enough of Ski at this point so, to shut him up, he had to respond or else risk hearing Ski talk shit for another hour.

A little while later, Sergeant Krall clicked onto the vehicle intercom and told us the convoy was beginning to move. Since we were in the middle, it took a few minutes before the domino effect kicked in. I looked behind us to watch as the long line of vehicles began to move and spit up dust into the air. We looked like one hell of a formidable fighting force.

The first half of the trip seemed to take the longest. After we had departed, we took a couple of turns before we got onto the main road. Each vehicle was keeping about thirty meters dispersion and varied its speed to avoid being hit by any improvised explosive devices.

From Camp Victory to the border of Kuwait and Iraq took about an hour. Kuwaitis drove by the convoy and waved. Some gave blank stares. The main thing I noticed was that almost everyone drove either a BMW or Mercedes, and they looked to be pretty new models too. Another thing that shocked me was that women were driving. During my first deployment to Iraq, I had never seen a woman drive a car. We were informed it was strictly forbidden in Iraqi culture. Seeing women driving in plain clothes took me by surprise.

The scenery wasn't much, but it was more pleasing to the eye than Iraq. From time to time, a small city would pop out of the desert. It seemed so odd to have countless miles of sand, and then suddenly a city with huge skyscrapers, and then nothing again. It wasn't as if there were surrounding suburbs.

The border was a sight to behold. At the crossing, there was a small building that held Kuwaiti and American soldiers. For miles on each side, there was concertina wire two wide and stacked two high to try to prevent any insurgents from crossing. In the front and back of the concertina-wire fence were large ditches.

The difference between the Iraqi side and the Kuwaiti side was very noticeable. The Kuwaiti side was very clean and orderly. On the Iraqi side, the charred remains of Iraqi military vehicles from the war were scattered about. There were even some abandoned vehicles that seemed as if nothing was wrong with them. Garbage was strewn about everywhere. Whereas Kuwaitis were driving brand-new Mercedes and BMWs, Iraqis were driving ragtag cars, trucks, and vans with the occasional antique Mercedes thrown in. To me, the difference was like night and day. Chills ran down my spine. Great, I thought, seven months in hell, and it begins now.

The guard at the border stopped the convoy to talk to the convoy commander. After words were exchanged, the convoy resumed its direction. The border guards gave us nods as each vehicle passed by as if to say, "Good luck out there." We needed as much of it as we could get.

I loved road marches back in the States because they were always nice and easy. As a scout, all I had to do was stand up and watch as cars drove by and people waved. However, Iraq was a different ballgame. Every hour, we would stop to conduct vehicle checks to ensure the vehicles could continue. During that time, the scouts had to dismount and provide security for the convoy. After about ten minutes, the scouts would remount the vehicles and resume the journey. This continued for about eight hours—eight long, boring, monotonous hours of standing. Sometimes we wouldn't even have time to go to the bathroom, so we had to use our empty water bottles to relieve ourselves, or if we were really bored and wanted to mess around, we'd open the back hatch of the vehicle slightly and piss through the crack onto the street as we drove. We would take turns standing up through the scout hatch so we could go to the bathroom. After a while, my legs ached and my skin felt as if it were roasting under the desert sun.

The sight of Camp Scania was like seeing Disney World for the first time. It seemed as if nothing had ever looked so good. We pulled the vehicles in to get refueled and then parked them at the staging point. Once the whole convoy had settled in and gotten to their correct positions, the vehicle commanders went to have a quick meeting with the convoy commander. In the meantime, everyone seemed to loosen up. People took out chairs and footballs. Some guys lit up cigarettes, and others put in a dip. The nervousness seemed to vanish for a bit.

Sergeant Krall came back about ten minutes later with the word. We were going to stay at Camp Scania for about two hours. During that time we needed to set up a fire watch (guard) on the vehicle. Once everyone was designated a time for fire watch, we set out to wreak havoc on Scania's chow hall and PX.

The thing about Army bases is that they are so much better than Marine Corps bases (unless it's an air base). Army bases have the best food, the best stores, and the best recreation centers. I met up with Corporal Jason "Tex" Sprenger, Sergeant Travis Madden, and a few others to go have chow. When we entered the chow hall building, we got the best food we could find, grabbed a soda and a bag of chips, and sat down to eat. The Army personnel looked at the whole group of Marines eating as if we were scavengers. We were nasty looking. We hadn't showered in days, we were covered in dust from the road march and, to top it all off, we were tearing into our food as if it were our last meal. I didn't care; I just wanted to fill up on some good food.

After we finished eating, we went our separate ways to find the PX, phones, or whatever else would occupy our time before we had to leave. I went back to my vehicle stuffed and happy and lay down by the tires to catch a quick nap.

Finally, everyone got the call to mount up. I checked to ensure all my team members were back and accounted for, and Sergeant Krall did the same with the crew. Once the convoy completed their radio checks, the convoy was on the move again.

Day turned to night. All vehicles were ordered to turn on their blackout lights. We continued to stop every hour to conduct vehicle checks. I donned my NVGs (night vision goggles) so I could get a better view of the surrounding area. The scenery was the same the whole way: garbage, broken-down vehicles, dead animals. It was such a sad sight to take in, especially knowing how privileged we are in the United States and how much we take it for granted.

Eventually, I switched positions with Forsyth, and I had Shearer do the same so we could rest our eyes. However, it wasn't much better sitting down than standing up. The scout compartment in the back of an LAV is approximately six feet wide and six feet long. It has two vertical doors on the back of the vehicle to let the scouts out and two horizontal hatches on top of the compartment for the scouts to stand up through. Running down the middle of it is a bench that faces both ways and takes up about two feet. So this leaves about two feet on either side of the bench for rifles, ammunition, gear, and legroom. I am six feet tall, and there is probably enough legroom, with everything else taken into account, for someone who is five feet tall. When all the gear and sea bags crammed into the scout compartment were taken into consideration, that room was cut in half. So it was an extremely uncomfortable sleep. My knees were up by my head. I was using my flak jacket as a headrest. My Kevlar helmet straps kept choking me. I was sweating profusely. I would have given anything at that moment for a nice feather pillow and a comfortable mattress.

After what seemed like an eternity, I was awakened by Forsyth asking to sit down. I got myself in order, grabbed my rifle, and let Forsyth take a nap. I looked over to Herman, who was still standing up, and I swear it seemed as if he was enjoying himself. I called over to him, and he turned around and gave me a big shit-eatin' grin and a thumbs-up. Good ol' Herman. He never seemed to care about anything; he just wanted to do his job and be done with it.

Around midnight, we met up with a few Army military police Humvees around the intersection of MSR Tampa and Mobile. They were assigned to escort us to Camp Baharia. Lucky them. A couple of the Humvees took up point, and the rest took rear security. The guys looked as if they were experienced. The gunners were low in their turrets, and they were constantly scanning. We new guys were exposing more than half of our bodies by standing up in the back and in the turrets. If an IED had exploded, it would have killed a whole crew.

It wasn't long before we passed the now-infamous Abu Ghraib prison. At night it was the most visible structure standing. It was lit up by a few floodlights. Concertina fences surrounded the whole encampment. Dirt mounds had been built to ward off any vehicle suicide bombers. To enter the compound, one had to go through a maze of obstacles that were placed to repel car bomb attacks. Guard towers were placed strategically around the base to provide the most protection. It was a virtual fortress, but one that was prone to many attacks.

From Abu Ghraib to Camp Baharia was only about eight miles, but it took us nearly thirty minutes to get there because of the slow speed at which we were traveling. Once we arrived at the road leading to the base, the Army MPs separated from our convoy, and we headed toward the base. Camp Baharia was adjacent to Camp Fallujah, the main Marine Corps stronghold in Fallujah. Both bases were less than a mile away from Fallujah, which was a major advantage for the insurgents.

As we approached our new home, the moon lit up the walls of the base. It looked completely deserted compared to Camp Fallujah. The only thing I noticed were a couple of Marines posted in the guard towers with their thermal sights scanning for any insurgents who were crazy enough to attack the base.

Great, I thought. Here we are stuck at the worst base in all of Iraq. Nothing that we had been told of the base was true. No place to sleep, no Burger King, no PX. Typical. What else did I expect? I was a Marine Corps grunt; we always got the short end of the stick.

# CHAPTER 9
# CAMP BAHARIA

Camp Baharia (Ba-ha-ree-a). It was originally named Camp Volturno, but shortly after we arrived, it was renamed Baharia specifically for the Marine Corps. In Arabic, the Marine Corps is called "mushaat al-baharia," which translates to "walkers of the navy," or naval infantry, so the name was very fitting.

The base used to be a retreat for one of Saddam Hussein's sons. It had a double wall surrounding it, with guard towers protruding from the wall about every hundred meters. In the middle of the camp was a huge, man-made lake with an amphitheater surrounding a portion of it. In the middle of the lake was an island with a few lampposts, none of which were lit.

The area around the entrance was deserted apart from the few Marines who were guarding it. Along the road that led to our section of the camp were a few small buildings that housed some of the headquarter elements for the other occupants of the camp, 2/1 (Second Battalion, First Marine Division) Marines. As we came closer to our section of the base, the road swerved. We passed a grouping of huts that seemed to have air-conditioning wall units. Everyone's spirits perked up a bit because we thought we were lucky enough to have a hard roof over our heads and some air conditioning. What the hell were we thinking? We were the Outlaws, we didn't get anything nice. Our company convoy slowly came to a halt in a giant patch of sand. Gunny Rossignol and Lieutenant Walker were guiding the vehicles into their designated areas.

Once the vehicles stopped, we dismounted and looked around. This giant patch of sand was what we were going to call home for the next seven months. It was about three football fields long and about a hundred yards wide. We were right next to the wall that was closest to Fallujah. Built into the wall were two cement buildings that were designated as the company headquarters and the staff and officer housing, both of which had air conditioning. The rest of us got to look forward to the dirt for the night.

After a long, tiresome trek to our new home, all we wanted was to sleep. We were told to take out our camouflage netting and set up a makeshift canopy to provide us with a little shade. We pulled out our poncho blankets and isomats and finally got a bit of well-deserved rest. Sand or not, it felt so good just to sit down and close my eyes.

We were awakened a few hours later by the blistering hot sun. I give the Iraqi people credit, I don't know how in the hell they deal with the extreme temperatures. In the winter months, it goes from eighty to ninety degrees during the day to fifty and below at night. The huge difference between day and night made packing for patrols and missions a pain in the ass.

A few Iraqi citizens were at our new home setting up two huge, circus-like tents. These were to be our new homes. The smaller of the two would house Headquarters

Platoon and some from Weapons Platoon, and the larger tent would house the remainder of Weapons Platoon and all of First, Second, and Third Platoons.

The problems with the tents were numerous and continued to haunt us through most of the deployment. First of all, the tents were about fifty feet high and resembled the giant tents used at the circus. They towered over the base walls and could be seen from Fallujah. An insurgent could easily use them as markers and set up an incredibly accurate mortar firing position. Fortunately, they were never that good. But this led to the next problem, which was that the tents were doused in flammable liquid to repel mosquitoes. So if a mortar did happen to land anywhere and a fire occurred, our tents would go up in a ball of flame in a matter of minutes. What made it even worse was that the tents provided shade from the sun, but they had no ventilation. So it ended up being more of a sweatbox than a place of rest. Also, it also had no flooring, so dust was constantly kicked up.

Next on the list of complaints was the chow hall, which was about a half-mile walk from our side of the base. It wasn't that bad of a walk; however, after an eight-hour patrol under the scorching hot sun, the last thing anyone wanted to do was walk to the chow hall. Plus, for a portion of the deployment, all they had to offer was t-rats (a vacuum sealed pre-cooked meal in a tray), which tasted worse than MREs.

The only good thing we had going for us was that we were close to the internet center. The internet center was a small hut with a couple of satellite dishes on top of it. It was our outlet to the rest of the world. It started out small, but by the time we left, it had everything it needed to support a battalion of Marines.

I looked at our tents and realized we had a lot of work ahead of us.

# CHAPTER 10
# CHANGEOVER

The Army personnel who had occupied our camp before us belonged to the Eighty-Second Airborne Division. There was also a small element from the Third Armored Calvary Regiment attached to them. They were a mechanized infantry regiment that was almost identical to us. Instead of light armored vehicles, they had the more common and well-known Bradley. The crews of the Bradley's were similar to the LAVs in that there was a gunner, a driver, and a vehicle commander. However, the scout compartment in a Bradley was able to hold six scouts, whereas the LAV could only hold four scouts comfortably.

We had only about two or three days to get ourselves situated before we had to start conducting missions. The first few were called left-seat-right-seat missions. These missions were to get the incoming relief (us) familiar with the territory, citizens, and patrol routes. The only people involved with these patrols were key personnel from the Outlaws: the platoon commanders, platoon sergeants, scout squad and section leaders, and some vehicle commanders. The Outlaw personnel would shadow their Army counterparts on the patrol and receive advice from them in everything from previous hostile encounters to the most common areas where improvised explosive devices were found. These missions lasted for about the first week to allow us to get accustomed to the area of operations and acquire a basic understanding of how everything worked.

The company's first taste of action came on one such mission. The Army personnel from the Eighty-Second Airborne Division decided it was time to introduce the Outlaw staff to the mayor of Fallujah and a few other key members. All of our officers went to this meeting except Lieutenants Walker and Rowell, who stayed behind to be the acting company commander and executive officer. If it weren't for sheer luck, they would have actually become the company commander and executive officer and the only officers left for the Outlaws.

The Eighty-Second Airborne Division would go into downtown Fallujah once a month to visit the local leaders of the community to discuss a variety of topics. In order for these meetings to take place with the maximum number of participants, they would have to announce the day and time a few days beforehand. This gave the insurgents ample time to set up ambushes. As a result, the Eighty-Second Airborne Division would bring a company of soldiers to secure the meeting place, placing snipers in strategic locations and setting up roadblocks, sentries, roving patrols, and aerial surveillance to provide maximum protection.

During the visit, Delta Company was allowed to bring one Humvee. Captain Shepard determined it would be best to bring a driver along with Lieutenants May, Snipes, and Nunnally. On the drive to the meeting place, it seemed as if the talk of ambush was a bit overdone.

The townspeople seemed friendly, kids were playing in the street, and there were no signs of insurgents anywhere. Once they arrived at the meeting area, the soldiers from Eighty-Second Airborne Division set up a defensive perimeter. As it was believed we would be conducting similar missions in the future, Captain Shepard and the lieutenants took notes on how everything was being done.

Two hours passed, and it seemed as if all the security measures were for nothing. Captain Shepard and the lieutenants became a bit bored and let down their guard. They broke open a few MREs to snack on and smoked a few cigarettes to kill the time.

Lieutenant Nunnally looked around at all the snipers that were positioned around the perimeter of the meeting place.

"This sure is boring," he said in a slight Texan accent. "I sure hope it gets a bit more exciting, or else these are gonna be really boring missions." The other lieutenants nodded in agreement.

Within a few seconds, the sound of mortars being fired in the distance could be heard.

BOOM! BOOM! BOOM!

The mortars began impacting around the meeting place. One landed just outside the defensive perimeter where a little boy was selling sandwiches, killing him instantly. Another round hit closer to home, landing on top of an outpost that housed a few Army and Navy snipers, wounding several of them. A third mortar landed harmlessly in a courtyard nearby.

After the mortars landed, all hell broke loose. Gunfire erupted from the south side of the defensive perimeter. The soldiers from the Eighty-Second Airborne Division began to engage them. With a desire to see some action, the lieutenants began to run toward a nearby building to get a better view of the firefight.

"Stop fuckin' running," Shepard yelled to the lieutenants. "The Army is gonna think you're a bunch of pussies if they see you running."

The lieutenants brought their run down to a brisk walk and continued toward the building. They had just stopped running when a mortar landed about twenty-five feet in front of them.

BOOM!

The sudden impact shocked the group of Outlaws and threw them off balance. A small piece of shrapnel kicked up and hit Lieutenant May in his eye. Fortunately, he was wearing his sunglasses, so the shrapnel lodged itself in the lens, just short of his eye. Nunnally felt a slight sting near his groin and looked down to see blood soaking his pants. Fearing the worst, he quickly began grabbing his crotch to make sure everything was still in place.

An Army medic who was nearby happened to look over in the direction of Nunnally and saw his blood-soaked pants. He ran over to Nunnally and began applying first aid.

Suddenly, gunfire erupted just north of their location. Lieutenants May and Snipes ran over to engage the insurgents while the medic continued taking care of Nunnally.

While Snipes and May were engaged, the medic had Nunnally position himself behind a Humvee for protection. Once they relocated, the medic had Nunnally stand up and remove his pants so the medic had better access to the wound. It just so happened that at that particular moment, Snipes and May looked back and saw Nunnally standing up with his pants down and the medic on his knees with his head close to Nunnally's crotch. It definitely provided a little humor in a tense situation.

The medic was eventually able to stop the bleeding by removing a small piece of shrapnel from Nunnally's thigh and plugged up the hole with a piece of gauze and a bandage. Later on, Nunnally would receive a Purple Heart for his wound, the first of many for the Outlaws.

When the entourage got back to the camp, they gathered us all around the COC (command operations center—the company office), to inform us of what they learned in Fallujah and what had happened during their brief encounter with the insurgents. Nunnally changed out of his blood-soaked pants and stood before us with a grin on his face. We broke into jokes about the situation, and eventually the staff gave us words of encouragement. Once the laughter died down, Captain Shepard told us what they had learned from their first engagement. We truly believed the enemy to be inaccurate and weak, unable to defeat us in battle.

The officers had their piece of the action, and now we wanted ours. We wanted to show these insurgents who was boss. We did in the long run, but we also came to respect our enemy. They weren't as brainless as we initially believed, and unfortunately it took lives to make us realize it.

# CHAPTER 11

# SANDBAGS

Those of us who were lucky, or unlucky in some cases, to stay back at the camp while these missions were being conducted had a lot of work in store for them. Our part of the camp needed a lot of work to make it livable. Gunny Rossignol was quite efficient at getting things in motion to establish a new home for us. Iraqi contractors started to build wooden floors in our tents to keep the dust from flowing around too much. Some were assigned to help these Iraqis in cleaning up the garbage that was left behind. Another big priority was to establish an ammo depot and set up our recreation tent, the maintenance tent, and the armory tent. We also needed to create a concertina fence around our parking lot. Before we acquired a shower trailer, we had only one place to take a shower, so a wooden gravity shower with a huge water tank, which didn't last very long, was built. Also, for a long time we had no clean port-a-johns, so we built two outhouses and a urinal. In order to keep the outhouses clean, someone had to empty out the cans where the crap went, which meant someone had to douse it in gasoline, burn it, and stir it to make it evaporate quickly. Additionally, everything needed to be fortified.

This was where the infamous sandbag working parties came in.

Gunny's second in command was the headquarters platoon sergeant, Sergeant Richard Jibson. Whenever people saw Sergeant Jibson walking toward their platoon's area or even close to their vicinity, everyone disappeared. Toward the middle of the deployment, he was nicknamed Bad News Jibbles by the lance corporals because almost every time he came over, he had to form a working party to do something, and it was most likely for sandbags. I'll give Sergeant Jibson his due: whatever he was tasked to do, he completed in a quick and timely fashion and to the best of his ability. Not only that, but he was really a nice guy. Unfortunately, the reputation of working parties followed him.

Just outside the perimeter of our little base was a large patch of sand that was extremely soft and had very little vegetation growing in it. This made it an ideal site to gather sand for the sandbags. What started off as a flat area of sand became a giant crater.

I don't know who supplies the military with sandbags, but the company must be making a fortune. Whoever they are, if they quit supplying them, a lot of junior enlisted Marines would be happy. Sandbag filling is comparable to the older military generation's punishment of peeling potatoes. We would spend countless hours digging and filling hundreds upon hundreds of sandbags for hours on end. It just sucks, and it's cruel punishment, especially under the boiling hot Iraqi sun.

The sandbag working party is feared mostly by the lance corporals and below, but non-commissioned officers (NCO), such as me, have been known to volunteer (or were "volun-told") to participate in these working parties. The equipment needed for this particular chore was sandbags and an e-tool (compact multi-tool that can act as a shovel). We would break into teams of two: one would hold the sandbag open and tie it when it was filled, and the other would shovel. The attire worn usually varied depending on the person and the temperature. Some would wear just their PT gear (shorts, T-shirt, and sneakers), others would wear boots, trousers, and a T-shirt, but no one ever dared to wear a full utility uniform or he would risk overheating.

There were side effects from doing the sandbag working party. Some were more serious than others, but they were all annoying. Overheating was probably the most serious, with some becoming too dehydrated and ending up in corpsman station, where they were administered an IV. Other lesser side effects included griping, sand in the eyes, congested nose from the sand, bad farmer's tan, and loss of time at the internet center or doing something else not involving work.

I would guess that we must have filled, at minimum, ten thousand sandbags. We filled sandbags for things that didn't even need it. We built a few bomb shelters, massive walls around both personnel tents, and walls around all of the headquarter tents. Sandbags held down the concertina fence and fortified the COC, the ammo dump, and many other things. It seemed as if every day we needed five hundred more sandbags for some new project Sergeant Jibson was tasked with.

We even tried to get around all the sandbags. We would double bag or stuff sandbags inside sandbags to make the pile go away. But just when we thought we had finished, someone else would come out with a few hundred more for us to fill. They were never ending.

Although many hated the sand pit, it was a place where the men made bonds and relieved stress. I would walk past the pit sometimes and listen to a group of Outlaws complaining about something: sandbags, NCOs, food, the weather—basically, anything that needed to be bitched about. But through all the complaining, I would always hear laughter or a joke. It formed a bond among the Marines because everyone had to do it, and everyone understood the pain involved in doing it. It also taught teamwork, something that was sorely needed in the beginning since most of us hardly knew one another.

When our relief arrived at the end of our tour, we were envious. From our viewpoint, they didn't need to build one more thing; we had done it all for them. All they needed to do was the maintenance and upkeep of the base. Lucky bastards. We had built them a sandbag fortress that could withstand an assault by a battalion's worth of insurgents.

Somewhere out there, at any given time, I know there is some junior Marine cussing under his breath or complaining with a group of his peers about how much he hates sandbags. The sandbag will forever be feared by many.

# CHAPTER 12
# IED INITIATION

One of the first missions we conducted just happened to be our rushed introduction to improvised explosive devices.

My platoon, also known as Red Platoon, was ordered to escort a convoy of Marines to an airbase in the western part of the Al-Anbar province called Camp "TQ" Taqqadum. We were all excited because we had heard good things about the camp. It had an internet center, good food, a nice PX, and other luxuries that our base lacked. It was also something different from the already-monotonous security patrols we had been doing, and it seemed like an easy mission.

Everything started off normal. The vehicles we were escorting were primarily seven tons (troop-carrying trucks). They were very lightly armored and not well equipped to engage the enemy. There were also a few Humvees interspersed throughout the convoy. Our platoon's vehicles took up key positions in the lead, middle, and rear of the patrol to provide the most security.

My vehicle was in the middle of the patrol. I was standing up through the scout hatch, as was my saw gunner, Shearer. We were both scanning the passing terrain looking for any signs of possible enemies or IEDs. Traveling at around forty miles per hour makes the task extremely difficult; nonetheless, we became slightly effective at spotting them. Some were easy to spot, such as those placed blatantly on the road, and others a bit more difficult, such as those dug into the side of the road, hidden in trash, or buried under rocks. However, all of our training never prepared us for our first experience.

We were coming up on one of the many overpasses along MSR Mobile. A few houses were scattered alongside the road, but what was most noticeable was the lack of people. No one was outside.

BA-BOOOOOOM!

"Holy shit!" I yelled to no one in particular. Shearer and I had both dropped to our knees inside of the scout compartment. Forsyth and Herman were trying to figure out what was going on.

"Everyone okay?" I asked. Herman and Forsyth gave me the thumbs up.

Once I made sure all my body parts were still attached, I stood back up to see what had happened. A huge smoke cloud surrounded a seven-ton that was about two hundred yards ahead of us close to the overpass. Parts of the vehicle littered the road.

"Scouts out!" Sergeant Krall yelled. I ordered my scouts out to form a hasty defensive perimeter around our vehicle as I went to Krall's location to find out what had happened and what he wanted us to do.

"What the fuck happened?" I yelled to Krall over the roar of the engines.

"A seven-ton up ahead with a platoon of Marines on it got hit by an IED," Krall yelled back. He was doing his best trying to talk to me while also listening to the radio traffic that was going on over the company communication network.

"They've got quite a few Marines wounded so we're gonna convert the 'L' into a medevac transport," he said before focusing his attention on the radio chatter again.

I looked back in the direction of the truck. Two LAVs took up defensive positions around the destroyed truck. The LAV-L (logistics vehicle) became the medical vehicle. Wounded Marines were being treated and loaded onto the LAV-L, the logistics variant of the LAV, to be rushed back to the hospital for further treatment.

The remainder of the convoy had broken into defensive positions alongside the road for about a quarter mile in either direction. The scouts from every vehicle were in defensive stances around their vehicles as their team leaders assessed the situation. Some Iraqi citizens had come out of their homes to see what had happened. A few Marines were questioning the people to find out if they knew who the triggerman was. Unfortunately, the insurgents blended in well, so we could never distinguish who the bad guy was. It was probably what was making this war the hardest for us. The citizens were never much help, either because they lived in fear of the insurgents or they hated us.

"Tanner!" Krall yelled, trying to get my attention. I turned to look back up at him. "They think they saw someone who could have been the triggerman running off in the distance so a team of scouts has been deployed in that direction. For now, set up your scouts in a defensive position."

I left the side of the vehicle and made my way to where I had positioned my scouts. I informed them of the situation and then sent them to either side of the road. I went to the left side of the road with my radioman, Forsyth, and I sent Shearer and Herman to watch over the right side. We did a hasty IED scan about two hundred meters from the road and set into our position to await further orders.

In time, Sergeant Krall called over the radio for Forsyth and me to meet back at the vehicle. I ran back as fast as I could with Forsyth trailing and met up with Krall. He told me that Lieutenant Snipes wanted my team to check out the two houses that were sitting off the right side of the road to see if there was anything suspicious. Forsyth and I ran over to Shearer and Herman, and we hurriedly got into a skirmishers formation to patrol the area on the way to the buildings.

The perimeter was surrounded by a low, mud-brick wall. The houses were about two stories tall and seemed to be deserted. Behind them was a giant palm grove that went on for a few acres. Garbage littered the property, and there was a broken-down car in the driveway.

As we approached the houses, Herman and Shearer called out that they saw someone run off into the woods. I got on the radio and gave Sergeant Krall a quick sitrep (situation report). He then passed the word onto Lieutenant Snipes, who sent a vehicle to survey the area.

In the meantime, I took my team to check out the remainder of the houses. We searched the car thoroughly for any contraband and then quickly inspected the outside of the houses. When we came up empty handed, we made our way back toward the LAVs. As we headed back, I noticed a man and a little girl approaching the house. We carefully approached them, and I began to question them with the little Arabic I had learned back in the States.

The Iraqi man informed me that the girl was his daughter. He had just come from somewhere else and knew nothing of what happened. He was friendly, but I was still suspicious. We searched him and found nothing. Since I only had a basic understanding of Arabic, I could never tell if someone was lying, so I was always on the cautious side. With nothing else to ask, we let them return to their home, and we headed back to the vehicle.

We set back into our defensive positions and lay there for another fifteen minutes before we got the call to mount up. We ran back to the vehicles, jumped in, and closed the doors. Shearer and I stood back up and scanned the area with a bit more attention. The explosion had suddenly put us on a new level of alertness.

Finally, the convoy continued on its road march but at a bit faster pace. We didn't need any more trouble along the way. The "L" and a couple other vehicles had headed back to the hospital to deliver the wounded Marines.

Nothing else extraordinary occurred on the journey, but the experience made us more aware of our surroundings. From what I was told, seven Marines were wounded in the vehicle. One shattered his leg, another broke his ankle, and the rest were riddled with shrapnel. I never knew who they were nor do I know what the overall outcome was, but my thoughts went out to them.

The improvised explosive device became our worst fear and deadliest enemy. We never underestimated it again. That was our first lesson in IED 101.

# CHAPTER 13
# FALLUJAH

We hadn't been in country for more than two weeks when we had our first major piece of action. On March 31, 2004, four American contractors were ambushed and killed, and their bodies were dragged through the streets of Fallujah and eventually hung from a bridge, with Iraqis rallying around them. This was just one of many incidents that led the bigwigs from MEF (Marine Expeditionary Force) Headquarters to decide they wanted to conduct a major assault on Fallujah. Their plan was to occupy the east side of the city to rout out the insurgents and gain a stronghold in Fallujah.

The Outlaws' job was to provide security on the roads surrounding the city and to conduct vehicle searches in hopes of finding insurgents fleeing. We were also trying to cut off all major escape routes for the insurgents. Our platoon was strategically positioned on the main road overlooking the northeast part of the city. The other platoons were located at various other points determined by the higher-ups. We had a few vehicles from Weapons Platoon attached to us as well as some elements from other units. Our headquarters element initially stayed back at the camp but was eventually brought forward to help with logistics and support.

The first few days of the assault were actually a bit boring since we didn't do much except search cars and conduct small patrols. The most exciting part of it was watching the "fireworks" display going on above the city at night. I could hear the occasional machine gun bursts from deep within the city. Sometimes there were a few tank rounds or artillery rounds fired into the city. From time to time, the insurgents would fire mortars in our general direction, and we would all run for cover. But overall, it was actually a bit boring. Hell, even the scout snipers got so bored that they decided to shoot the light bulbs that were illuminating the MSR at night. It was actually amusing to watch them do it because it took quite a few shots to knock them out. For some reason, even after they shot them, they continued to glow, which seemed to frustrate the hell out of the snipers.

Nighttime was probably the eeriest part of the day. After dusk, the Muslim clerics would chant verses, songs, and sayings from the Qur'an over the loudspeakers that were attached to their mosque towers. Our interpreters would tell us that some of the things that the clerics were saying were anti-American. They would tell their followers to attack us, kill us, or not aid us in our mission. It wasn't really what they were saying that made it so creepy; it was the sound of the teachings that made it disturbing. Dusk would come, and one by one each mosque would come to life with a spine-chilling song preaching hatred toward Americans. And then as suddenly as it came, it stopped, and there was silence.

After the prayers were over, Psy-Ops (Psychological Operations) would sometimes patrol the roads. Once we found out what they were doing, it became a bit entertaining. They had Humvees with huge loudspeakers on the top. Occasionally, they would have a prerecorded message asking the law-abiding citizens of Fallujah to inform us where the insurgents were or to stay inside so they didn't get shot. Every now and then they would also drive by playing AC/DC or some other heavy metal band extremely loud in an attempt to unnerve the enemy. I don't know if it ever worked, but I sure enjoyed the music.

A couple of days into the assault, we were reassigned to conduct vehicle checkpoints farther down the MSR and along the ASRs (alternate service routes). We never really found much. Once in a while we found a pistol or rifle, but we didn't find many. We couldn't even confiscate them unless it could be used as an explosive.

Part of what made the insurgency so effective was that they constantly adapted to every new technique we tried. We started conducting numerous vehicle checkpoints, so they devised another way to smuggle weapons to the city; they used the Red Crescent (non-Christian counterpart to the Red Cross) vehicles. Somehow, the enemy figured out that we hardly ever searched Red Crescent vehicles because we believed them to be for humanitarian assistance within the city. They were mostly deemed off limits by the higher-ups. So the insurgents decided to use our weakness of humanitarian assistance against us.

One such day, word was passed over the company "net" (radio frequency) that there was a convoy of Red Crescent vehicles entering our vicinity heading toward the Jordanian hospital on the outskirts of Fallujah. It was said that there was the possibility of weapons mixed in with the cargo. This was stated because other Red

Crescent vehicles had been stopped earlier that day with huge caches of weapons.

About ten minutes had gone by when the vehicles finally came into view. At first glance they looked like oversized farm trucks used to carry sheep. As they came closer, it was a funny sight to behold because they reminded me of a mix between old farm trucks and circus cars. There were four trucks that were about twenty feet tall, with tarps covering the top to stop cargo from flying out. Leading the "convoy" was a small ambulance with the Red Crescent painted on the side. Sitting on top of the cabs of the vehicles were anywhere between one to three Iraqis, and inside each cab were another three Iraqis.

My vehicle (Red 2) and Sergeant Richard Learn's vehicle (Red 4) were tasked with stopping and searching the rear vehicles while the other section of our platoon searched the front trucks. We brought them to a halt and had the Iraqis dismount the vehicles. I ordered my team to set up a civilian search area where Forsyth and Shearer would search the Iraqis while Herman and I searched the trucks. Lance Corporal Duarte's (Red 4 team leader) team followed suit on the other vehicle. After thoroughly searching both vehicles, Duarte and I started to question the passengers. Fortunately, some of them were doctors and could speak passable English.

While we were talking to them, I felt uneasy because a few of them didn't seem to be doctors or nurses. Some gave hardened stares like that of a soldier and whispered among themselves. They eyed us suspiciously but didn't make direct eye contact, as if they were avoiding something. They were also the ones who didn't speak English. The doctors told us that they were nurses and helpers, but that still didn't ease our suspicions. However, even though our alarms were raised, we had nothing to hold them on and had to let them pass.

Luckily, we had done a very thorough search and found nothing. Nevertheless, about an hour later, another convoy of Red Crescent trucks was searched near the hospital and had weapons mixed in with the medicine. This was getting to be a more complicated war than we had anticipated.

# CHAPTER 14
# AMBUSH ALLEY

After a few days' worth of what seemed like endless vehicle checkpoints and patrols, our company's mission changed. We were to go to the western edge of our area of operations, which was a bridge we had nicknamed the Tar-Tar Bridge. We had to set up security positions there and conduct small patrols out of the area, set up more vehicle checkpoints, and provide security for military convoys going through.

The first couple of days and nights were relatively boring. Our platoon would go out at the same time every day and conduct short patrols along the ASRs and survey the area around the bridge and truck stop. Occasionally, we would conduct vehicle checkpoints along the MSR and stop cars at random. It became very monotonous. Second (White) Platoon got called on to support some other MEF mission at the time. Third (Blue) Platoon was requested to be attached to another battalion as a support element. So that left our platoon, Headquarters (Black), and Weapons (Brown) Platoons to conduct these security patrols.

Around the night of April 6, things began to get a bit more lively. That night we were settled into a defensive position close to the bridge in a defensive 360.

I could have sworn I saw my breath, but I think my mind was playing tricks on me. None of us had prepared for the huge temperature variation, so most of us were only wearing our camouflage utilities with a T-shirt underneath. That night for fire watch, we had gone down to 50 percent, meaning only half of the team had to stay up for watch while the other half rested. I was lying in the prone position behind a small mound of dirt shivering uncontrollably (the temperature during the day was somewhere around eighty degrees, and it suddenly dropped to fifty), and Shearer was to the far right of me doing the same. Every fifteen minutes or so, I would slowly get up to check on Shearer to see if he needed anything. He just griped about how damn cold it was and how he couldn't wait to get into his sleeping bag. After an hour on watch and an hour left to go, I couldn't take it anymore. I ran over to my vehicle to get my camouflage poncho blanket out of my rucksack (backpack) and got Shearer his too. I went back to my position, covered myself with the blanket, and sat there for a while, constantly scanning the horizon and checking on Shearer to see if he was staying awake and all right. I just couldn't wait for my two-hour shift to be over so I could bundle up in my sleeping bag and get warm again.

A little while later, I heard a convoy driving by our position on the main road in blackout conditions (no lights on at all; they drive using night-vision goggles). This had been happening for the past few days with no problems, so it didn't seem new. They passed, and I went back to my normal routine—scan and check, scan and check.

That's when it happened.

BOOM! RATA TAT TAT RATA TAT TAT!

The convoy that had just gone by drove maybe two miles past our position and came under fire. The convoys, however, only returned fire but did not pursue the enemy. From what I understand, if a convoy were to come under enemy fire, the convoy was to return fire but speed up to pass through the enemy fire and then request backup.

The night was filled with parachute flares and green and red tracers. It reminded me of the Fourth of July in Staten Island when I was a kid. And then, as suddenly as it happened, it stopped. There was complete silence. We were ordered to stay in place, and that is exactly what we did—just sat and waited, which was extremely unnerving.

About a half hour went by, and another convoy passed. The same thing happened. They got about two miles down the road from us, and the fireworks started going off. And once again, we did nothing.

An hour passed with no sounds to be heard. Another convoy passed, and as was becoming the routine, it came under fire and they ran like hell to get out of the enemy fire.

Finally, MEF Headquarters gave us the order to check it out and see what was going on down there. Captain Shepard decided to send just our platoon to check out the situation and report back. Sweet. We finally get to do something new, I thought.

"Scouts in!" yelled Krall.

It was an eerie sight. One by one the scouts stood up, appearing to materialize out of the darkness, and ran to their vehicles to mount up. I could feel the excitement in the air. We knew we were going to get some action, something we had been looking forward to since we first landed in Kuwait.

We all loaded up, and the vehicles took off and headed east on MSR Mobile. My vehicle and Lieutenant Snipes' vehicle were off to the left-hand side of the MSR in the sand, and the other two vehicles were on the right-hand side of the road. I donned my NVGs to get a better view of the surrounding area. Shearer was popped up in his scout hatch next to me doing the same. He released his bipods and let the submachine gun rest on the scout hatch. My other two scouts were anxiously sitting in the scout compartment wondering what was going on and hoping to get in on some of the action.

We arrived at our destination, and we couldn't see anything. The vehicles came to a halt to scan the area in their thermal sights. Still nothing. We resumed our vehicular patrol for another half a mile.

PFFFFFFFFFFFFTTT BOOM!

A RPG (rocket propelled grenade) came out of thin air and hit Red 4 in the buzzle rack (which is attached to the turret).

"Contact right!" I yelled over the sound of the explosion. All around us, gunfire suddenly erupted from both sides of the road.

There was no communication from Red 4 for a few seconds after the explosion. I was worried because my best buddy, Tex, was the gunner, and a few of my good friends were scouts in that vehicle. It continued moving forward, but there was still no communication.

Luckily, only the communication radio had been knocked out of place, and the wires had come loose. Tex had flipped the radios over to internal communication and had Duarte communicate with the other vehicles with his man pack (PRC-119). Phew, I thought, that was a close call. My adrenaline was pumping now, and I was looking all over the place to acquire a target.

Our section rolled back up onto the road and formed a tactical column with the other section. RPGs were flying all over the place, some just barely skimming overhead and missing the vehicles by inches. Shots were being fired from all over. It was utter mayhem. The funny thing is I wasn't scared at all. For some people, this sounds crazy, but until you're actually in the line of fire, you really have no idea how you're going to act. Maybe it was the way we were trained as Marines, or perhaps I was just so much of a video game first-person shooter junkie that I actually looked forward to the combat. It was actually very exhilarating, an adrenaline rush.

Suddenly, the beautiful sound of the LAV 25 mm Bushmaster chain guns sang in harmony.

Boom Boom Boom! Boom Boom Boom!

There was nothing better than to hear that wonderful sound when we were in a tight situation. The cannons spit death and were nearly unstoppable. During the initial invasion of Iraq, Iraqi combatants feared the LAV, and because of this, they were given a special name in Arabic. The English translation of the name was eight-wheeled destroyers.

I loaded a parachute flare into my grenade launcher and let it rip. The sky burst into an eerie white glow. I could see some of the insurgents propped up on the hills along the road. I watched in shock as a few RPGs come fairly close to our vehicle. A few exploded just before or just after some of the vehicles.

Once I identified some insurgents, I stood up higher in the scout hatch, exposing half of my body, and started to shoot round after round from my M-16A4/M203. Shearer was next to me letting off seven-round bursts from his submachine gun. From time to time, I would fire off a grenade from my launcher. In the meantime, the LAVs were still spitting death. As we passed by each group of insurgents and unloaded on them, the return fire would stop and be replaced with nothingness. We'd then refocus on another pocket of resistance farther ahead.

And then we got to a certain point on the road where everything just stopped, and there was silence. We reloaded everything we had, and Lieutenant Snipes turned the platoon around for round two. We headed west again on the same road to assess the damage we had brought upon the insurgents. And once again we came under heavy fire. This same routine repeated three more times. We would drive west or east and come under fire, engage the enemy, get to the end of the road, reload, and come back through again. The routine finally stopped when we went through and not a shot was fired. Apparently, they got the hint. Don't mess with a group of amped-up Marines and their LAVs.

After our final pass by that section of the road, we came to the conclusion that the enemy had set up in small pockets across the road from one another as if they were in a tactical column placement. It was an ingenious setup, allowing them to engage us from both sides and causing a bit of confusion.

When we got back to our temporary base, we were all ranting and raving about how we did this and that, bragging how many grenades we shot off and how many insurgents we took out. The gunners were arguing over who engaged first, and the vehicle commanders were bragging about whose gunner was more accurate.

"Dude, I went through nearly three hundred rounds of ammo and used six of my 203 grenades," I overheard Duarte say to his saw gunner, Lance Corporal Thornton.

"Yeah, I used nearly two drums of ammo," Thornton proudly stated.

I looked over at Shearer. "How much did you go through?"

"All three drums. What about you?"

"Used about two hundred rounds, a couple of my 203 grenades, and a few of the parachute flares. That was some crazy shit, huh?" I asked with a big, shit-eating grin plastered on my face.

"Hell yeah it was. I hope we get to go out there tomorrow and do that again."

"Yeah, that'd be pretty sweet." I went back to cleaning my rifle and thought about how exhilarating the whole experience was.

Eventually, after briefing Captain Shepard on the encounter, Lieutenant Snipes came over to give us a brief overview of what had happened, how we handled it, and what we could do better next time—better known in the military as an after-action report. Once he was done debriefing us, we got the command to hunker down and get some well-deserved sleep.

The next morning I awoke still psyched about the day before. I'm a combat-tested Marine, I thought. Everyone else seemed to be thinking the same thing.

Stories were still being told as we got ourselves organized for the next day of patrols.

Sometime that afternoon some sad news was passed to our platoon. Our scout section leader, Sergeant Jeffrey Lesher, had to be sent back to the States because his mother was ill and needed assistance, and he was the only one who could do it. That left us one experienced man short of a full platoon, and his position was left open. As I had shown myself capable of the responsibility of being a section leader, Lieutenant Snipes appointed me to the position. I was to stay on Red 2 until we got back to Camp Baharia, where we could sort all the details out. But I was officially a scout section leader. Boy, could my day get any better. First an adrenaline-pumping firefight, and then a promotion. Things were looking up.

We were given a debriefing of the previous night's events and then went back to our daily operations. We honestly thought that was the last of the action. However, the same thing happened for the next three nights. Same routine, same place, except each time we went through, it didn't seem as if they had as much ammo or as many people as the last time. After about the fifth day, nothing happened in that area again.

We stayed in that general vicinity for another two weeks, until the first assault on Fallujah was over. For the remainder of our time in Iraq, there was never any disturbance in that area. But in our minds and on our maps, that area will remain with us forever. We had a new name for it.

Ambush Alley.

# CHAPTER 15
# STAR LIGHT

It's amazing the things we did to keep our minds off the day-to-day happenings and bring hope to our lives. We would tell jokes, play games, write letters, and watch movies—anything to forget about what was going on around us. If you didn't pick up some kind of hobby, routine, or ritual, the madness would begin to consume you.

I know that a few of us started rituals or routines before going on patrols or right after coming back. Some would pray for protection of themselves and their friends, others kept something lucky with them, like a picture, and a few had other superstitious routines they had to go through before and after the patrol. I had my own, which helped me stay semi-sane and gave me a little bit of hope.

One day, while relaxing after a patrol in our platoon's section of the hooch, I decided to watch *Glory*, a Civil War movie with Morgan Freeman. The part that stuck with me the most was what the group of African American soldiers did one night. They all gathered around a campfire and broke into some kind of gospel song and chant. The group of men would hum the music while an individual would chant about something or other. After he was done preaching, the group would then break into song, singing "Oh my lord, lord, lord, lord," and then go back to humming again. I have no idea why this particular part of the movie was stuck in my mind, but I incorporated it into some of my daily rituals.

The next patrol we went on was like the rest: same old stuff, different day. However, when we got back onto base and were driving toward the parking lot, I broke into a smile, started a little drumbeat by thumping my hand on the scout hatch, and began to sing the chant that I had seen in the movie. Lance Corporal Shearer, who had also seen the movie, instantly recognized the song and got into it with me. He started grazing his hand on the scout door in resemblance of a tambourine or cymbal. We would pick up the beat and then slow it down; one of us would belt out some kind of song while the other provided backup. Lieutenant Snipes's vehicle was behind us, and he was shaking his head wondering what the hell had gotten into us. So there we were, two Marines covered in dust and sweat, singing and dancing and preaching to no one in particular but having a good time. I believe it was some kind of stress reliever for us. For as long as I remained on that vehicle, Shearer and I would sing the same song each day as we came back from patrol. Good times, as we liked to say.

*****

I was never a religious man; I wasn't raised in a religious house nor ever went to church. I don't really believe in anything; however, I was a little superstitious and had some weird traditions that I took from religion.

One in particular was Buddhism. When I was a child living in Staten Island, my father had a cement statue of Buddha sitting on our back porch. It was marked with holes from erosion and was more of a decoration than anything else. My father would sometimes rub its belly and tell us that when we did that, it would bring us good luck. So every once in a while when I passed Buddha, I would rub his belly hoping for good luck. I took that bizarre tradition with me to Iraq.

At one of the Army bases we visited in Iraq, I found a small wooden statue of Buddha for sale. Seeing that I hadn't brought one with me on this deployment, I decided to buy it. I brought it back to the hooch and put it on my makeshift dresser, where it stayed the whole time. Before we went on a mission, I would make sure to rub Buddha's belly for good luck, and then I would force my buddy Tex to do the same thing. He probably thought I was nuts, but I assured him it would bring us good luck. I have no idea if it ever did, but it helped put my mind at ease.

I brought another custom with me from my childhood. Each night, whether we were going on patrol, coming back, or doing nothing, I would stand outside my hooch and look up at the stars. I've always been able to look up into the sky and see stars, but you've never seen the night sky until you've been in the middle of a desert with no light pollution. It's absolutely amazing how many stars you see. It's as if every piece of the sky was lit up with millions of stars. It sounds childish now, but I would recite the children's rhyme "Star light, star bright, first star I see tonight" and then make a wish. But instead of making a wish, I would pick one star in particular and "send" my thoughts to it. I liked to believe that someone I knew back home was looking at that same star and would receive my message and know that I was doing well. I would ask the stars for protection of my platoon and me, ask them to ensure my family and friends stayed safe, and thank them for the previous day's help. I made sure I did this every night because I feared that if I didn't, something bad would happen. I don't believe it ever really helped, but it was my way of relieving stress and hoping for the best for all of us.

There is a saying that in war, everyone finds God. I never found him, but I did find a way to get stuff off my chest. Crazy or not, it helped.

# CHAPTER 16
# TATTOO

The Outlaws' first significant casualty happened only a few weeks into our deployment. Not belittling the injuries that First Lieutenant Nunnally sustained, but the wounds he took were minor in comparison to what others endured. I wasn't present when the incident occurred, but I was able to see some footage of the firefight as well as hear many of the stories that were brought back that day, and believe me, it's definitely a great story to tell.

On April 8, 2004, Blue Platoon (Third) was conducting an escort mission for an Army truck platoon. They had to escort a bunch of vehicles from Taji Airfield base to Camp Fallujah. It seemed like any other mission: one hell of a long, boring road patrol escorting vehicles from one point to another. That particular day, as the convoy was traveling west toward Camp Fallujah, a few civilian eighteen-wheelers had stopped because something happened to be blocking the road. Blue 2, the lead vehicle of the convoy, pushed forward to assist the civilians in removing the obstacle. As soon as he got close, insurgents appeared from nowhere and ambushed the vehicles, peppering them with RPGs and gunfire.

As most of the civilians did when they encountered an ambush, they tried to flee rather than stick around for the fight. Sure, they may not have had the firepower to do anything, but more often than not, they do more damage when they flee than if they just stay put. And, of course, they did damage. The drivers of the eighteen-wheelers jumped back up into their rigs and tried to back up and hightail it out of there. But due to the small amount of room to maneuver and the constant barrage of enemy fire, two of the rigs jackknifed, two others were disabled by the gunfire, and an LVS (a flatbed-type military truck used for hauling equipment and vehicles) took a round into its gas tank, totally disabling it. The drivers jumped out and headed for cover while Blue Platoon began to engage the insurgents. Unfortunately, this cut off Blue 2 from the rest of the platoon.

Sergeant Callendar, a medium height, no-nonsense kind of guy and the vehicle commander of Blue 2, immediately took charge of the situation and had his scouts engage the insurgents that were encroaching. I still remember seeing some of that footage, and I could hear the scouts screaming out, "Get some" and having a hell of a good time. You could even hear Lance Corporal Wheeler with his thick Boston accent screaming "Eat that!" as he shot round after round at the enemy's position. I got an adrenaline rush just hearing it. Sergeant Callendar then had his gunner, Corporal Bradley Swenson, focus on taking out the RPG positions with the LAV 25 mm Bushmaster gun. While Swenson was blasting away at the RPG teams, Callendar popped out of his hatch and started picking off insurgents with his 240G pintle-mounted machine gun. At one point, he took some shrapnel to his hand, but it barely fazed him, the adrenaline was pumping too hard, and the last thing he needed to focus on was a small flesh wound.

Meanwhile, the rest of the platoon had come under fire. Second Lieutenant Rowell's vehicle, Blue 1, started to come under attack from both sides of the road. Callendar had his scouts provide cover for Rowell while Rowell's scouts engaged the insurgents who were trying to trap them.

A little over halfway through the firefight, a quick reaction force (QRF) of M1A1 tanks was sent out to assist Blue Platoon in defeating the insurgents. The tanks started blasting away at the insurgents' positions. Each time a round fired out of one of those beasts, you'd hear a big boom, and a short distance away someone or something was decimated. Callendar took this as an opportunity to get the drivers of the eighteen-wheelers back into their vehicles so they could get them out of the kill zone. The insurgents must have seen this happening because as soon as the big rigs began to move, several RPGs were fired all at once, spraying the LAVs and tanks with shrapnel. Just like before, Callendar and the rest of Blue Platoon engaged the insurgents, trying their best to subdue them while the civilians made their exit. Two of the rigs were able to head back in the direction they had come from, but there were still two disabled vehicles. Blue Platoon and the tank platoon surrounded the disabled vehicles waiting for additional support to take the disabled trucks away. This was when disaster struck.

Sergeant Callendar, still fighting off insurgents with his 240G machine gun and with his body half exposed, was struck by a 7.62 mm round on the right side of his chest. Somehow the bullet managed to hit the exact spot where there was no protection from the vest, and the bullet went clear through his chest, coming out the other side and lodging into the back of his vest. Callendar spit up blood, and it began to drool from his mouth, dripping from his chin. Wiping it away, he called over to Rowell that he had been hit and was spitting up blood. Rowell instructed him to maneuver his vehicle so he could meet up with the corpsman, Doc Ferguson, to receive first aid.

Callendar finally got his vehicle into position and slowly got out of his turret. He climbed down to the side of the LAV, and Ferguson began to strip him down so he could attend to the wound.

This next part will forever stick with me and will attest to how bad-ass Callendar was. With blood coming out of the side of his mouth and having one hell of a hard time breathing, Callendar calmly started asking Ferguson questions.

"Doc, did the bullet exit my body?" Callendar asked between breaths.

"Yeah, it came out of your lower back," Doc calmly said.

"Did it go through my tattoo? I'm gonna be fucking pissed if it did." No care in the world for his life, all he wanted to do was make sure that the tattoo dedicated to his wife wasn't desecrated. Awesome.

"No man, it's fine," Ferguson responded with a chuckle.

Callendar started to feel a bit of the pain and noticed his breaths were becoming a bit harder to take.

"Doc, did it do any damage to my lungs?" Callendar asked.

Ferguson was hesitant to answer. He didn't want to say anything that wasn't true nor did he want to freak Callendar out.

"Listen Doc, I think it punctured my lung. It kinda feels like it. What do you honestly think?"

"Yeah, I think it might have done some damage," Ferguson said with obvious concern in his eyes. "Wheeler," Ferguson turned and yelled over the ongoing commotion "come over here and talk to Sergeant Callendar. I don't need him to go into shock."

Lance Corporal Jason Wheeler who had been videotaping some of the events of the day came running over and started nervously talking. "It's friggin' hot out here. I can't wait to get home where the weather..." Wheeler started to say in his thick Boston accent.

Callendar quickly interrupted him. "Stop talking to me about bullshit, Wheeler. Let's talk about something normal." Wheeler quickly pulled himself together and collected his thoughts. "Sorry Sergeant," he said, "it was the first thing that came to mind. So, you and your wife figure out what you're gonna name the baby when he's born?"

The question seemed to come out of nowhere and took Callendar by surprise. The whole time he was worrying about his Marines, he never once thought about the little baby boy his wife and he were expecting.

"No, we haven't really figured it out yet," Callendar responded, still trying to grasp the concept that if he didn't live through this, his little boy would be fatherless.

Fortunately, the bullet did not take Callendar's life. When a medivac arrived at the scene a few minutes later, Callendar stood up on his own will and slowly, with some help from his fellow Outlaws, walked to the helicopter. He was later taken back to the States to receive the proper care he needed and received a Bronze Star for his efforts. He damn well deserved it too. Watching the whole scene unfold on the video was motivating as hell. Seeing how Callendar handled it in such a calm way was inspiring. I'm truly glad he was able to make it through. Thankfully, his tattoo made it through in one piece too. The only thing worse than a crazed-up, suicidal insurgent is a pissed-off wife.

# CHAPTER 17
# BAD KARMA

Of all the information the Army unit passed on to us, one thing struck me as strange: a town by the name of Al Gharma (Ga-ar-ma), nicknamed Bad Karma by the Army. The Army unit told us that whenever they rode through the town, they closed all the hatches on the vehicles and drove as fast as possible to avoid any confrontations. Supposedly, the small farming town was a huge insurgent hideout, and whenever Americans would drive through, they would open fire with anything and everything they had. When we took over the area of operations, we decided that we weren't going to follow the same procedure; we weren't going to allow the insurgents to dictate how we worked. So one day it was decided that the company would start doing limited patrols into the town and around the outskirts of it.

Second Platoon was the first platoon to take on this new challenge. They only had three vehicles since one was down for repairs, so they added an LAV-L and equipped it with an extra M-240G submachine gun. The whole crew from the broken-down vehicle boarded the "L," arming the vehicle with an extra four M-16s for more firepower since the vehicle didn't have a 25 mm gun. The purpose of their patrol was only to survey the town, but they had a lot more in store for them.

On their first patrol, they had been patrolling around the area for only a few minutes before they were fired upon. So they engaged the enemy in their own territory and began entering the town. The streets were narrow, which hindered the ability of the LAVs to effectively engage and maneuver. There were man-made roadblocks, snipers on the roofs, IEDs, and many other things that were dangerous to White Platoon. However, no matter what obstacle was in their way, they were still able to decimate the enemy and accomplish their mission.

They were extremely lucky, too. When the platoon finished their eight-hour shift, most of which was spent in Bad Karma, they came back to tell their war stories about how they had done this and that. Some of the stories may have been a bit embellished, but after hearing many of them and getting a few honest accounts from some of my friends in White Platoon, I was able to figure out that they had one hell of a time and had accomplished their mission. Not only did they have their stories, they had some evidence to back it up. After further examination of the vehicles, I could see marks all over the vehicles where bullets had hit the armor and bounced off. Some of the marks were extremely close to where the scouts in the back had been. A few inches higher and they may not have been bragging as much. However, they did a great job and deserved the credit they received.

Third Platoon was next in line to test out Bad Karma. They went out immediately after White Platoon returned to assess the situation in the town. From what was passed on to us, they saw that the insurgents had refortified the town with more barricades that were designed to block the vehicles in the city. They also found more IEDs and saw insurgents running around getting ready for the next possible assault.

Blue Platoon approached the town the same way as White Platoon did. And just like White Platoon, Blue Platoon received fire from all over. Their vehicles blew up the roadblocks and avoided all the possible IEDs. They blew up vehicles and engaged the enemy on their turf. The firefight went on for a while, and eventually, after no more shots were heard, they pulled out of the town to continue the surveillance of Gharma.

After hearing the news of White and Blue Platoon's firefights, we were itching to go in and get our hands dirty. Lieutenant Snipes and Staff Sergeant Phelps gathered us around to give us the mission briefing and to ensure we all knew what our duties were and how we were going to conduct the assault. We were all psyched and ready to go. We had already had our first taste of action, but we were jealous of the other platoons; we wanted our own stories to tell and our own vehicle scars to prove it.

We added more ammunition to the vehicles and prepped ourselves for a long firefight. I loaded up with six magazines of 5.56 mm ammunition for my rifle and put eight 40 mm grenades in my pouches for my grenade launcher. I had my new team prep the same way, having PFC Zabala ready his rifle, Doc Barajas ensure his medical equipment was filled and accessible, and Lance Corporal Redd get the SMAW (Shoulder Launched, Multi-Purpose Assault Weapon, a.k.a. rocket launcher, a.k.a. one bad-ass piece of weaponry) prepped for taking out roadblocks or other potential hazards.

Soon we were off to rendezvous with Blue Platoon. We met them at a small field on the outskirts of the town. We pulled our vehicle up next to one of Blue's vehicles, and the scouts dismounted to take up the positions of Blue's scouts. I closed the back door of the vehicle and met up with a few of the other scouts from Blue Platoon to find out what had happened. My two friends, Lance Corporals Jason Wheeler and Pat Walsh, were both going on about their firefight and what they had seen and everything they had done. It seemed as if they were talking a mile a minute. Staff Sergeant Phelps and the vehicle commander we had parked next to exchanged words, and when they finished, Walsh, Wheeler, and the other scouts of the vehicle loaded up and prepared to head back to base.

In the meantime, I placed my scouts in good defensive positions and met up with Staff Sergeant Phelps to find out what the new word was. He told me we were going to wait for dawn and then set up closer to the town and recon it for a bit. Then we would eventually enter the city as the other platoons did. He also warned me that the city was blockaded again by the insurgents, some of the vehicles on the side of the roads in town were booby trapped, snipers had created bunkers on the tops of buildings, and IEDs lined some of the roads. For a split second, nervousness crossed my mind, but I brushed it off quickly and informed my scouts of the current situation.

Blue Platoon's vehicles headed back to the base, and we moved from our positions to get a closer look at the city. We crossed a main road and settled in about one kilometer away from Al Gharma. Corporal Klinger passed over the radio that he saw a man-made roadblock on the main road into the town. He noticed a few people walking around the town carrying weapons and setting up defenses. The problem with the blockades was that if they were used correctly, they would corner us into a trap where we would get destroyed. So Lieutenant Snipes came up with a new plan. He wanted to use the SMAW to destroy the blockades while the LAV-25 chain guns engaged enemy fortifications.

He passed his idea over the platoon net and got a favorable response, so his next decision was to figure out who was going to shoot it. In the platoon, there were only three experienced SMAW gunners: Lance Corporal Duarte, Lance Corporal Redd, and myself. Redd had the most experience, so I suggested his name to Staff Sergeant Phelps, which would allow me to stay with my team and manage them properly if we were to engage in combat. Phelps passed Redd and Duarte's name onto Lieutenant Snipes, but he rejected them and asked for me to come over to his vehicle to use the SMAW on the blockades. I was honored and exhilarated, but also a bit upset because I wanted to stay with my team when it all went down. Phelps asked Snipes to reconsider Redd for the position, but Lieutenant Snipes was determined to have me take it out. So I slung my rifle on over my shoulder, grabbed the SMAW and a prepped rocket, and ran over to Lieutenant Snipes's vehicle.

After running for about a quarter of a mile to meet up with his vehicle, I was a bit out of breath. I looked up at Lieutenant Snipes, and he had a big grin on his face. It definitely made me laugh a bit and made me remember why he got his nickname "Turtle" from Shearer and me. When Lieutenant Snipes had all of his gear on (flak jacket, CVC helmet, and glasses), he looked like a giant turtle. When he shrugged his shoulders, it looked like a turtle retreating into his shell. Of course when I teased him about it, he teased me about everything else in return, but it was all in good fun.

After all joking was put aside, he told me that I was going to load up into his vehicle and we were going to pull up within two to three hundred meters of the town. When we got into position, they would lay down covering fire while I jumped out of the back and released a rocket into the blockade. It sounded like something straight out of the movies. I kept on envisioning myself jumping out, dropping to the ground, legs spread apart like the guy from *Desperado* and firing off one bad-ass rocket and obliterating the enemy.

The only thing holding us back from going in right then was that we were waiting for a call from company headquarters permitting us to continue on as scheduled. We waited for what seemed like a half hour before word came back. The mission was a no-go. They completely dropped the mission on us for a reason still unknown to me. Talk about an adrenaline kill. Everyone in our platoon was psyched to go in, to get some action, to have a story, but it was canceled. I could see in Lieutenant Snipes' eyes that he was just as pissed as the rest of us.

Instead, we were ordered to continue on our routine counter-IED and counter-mortar patrol. The rest of the day was just a blur because our spirits were down. We got back to base, and people were asking us about our assault. We just brushed them off and continued on with our daily routines. At that moment, it just seemed as if we were the unwanted child of the company, as if everyone else got to have a piece of the pie but we were left with crumbs.

"Maybe another time" was what we were told.

# CHAPTER 18
# HUMPTY DUMPTY

Only a couple of days went by before the MEF Headquarters decided it was time to put an end to the problems in Gharma. We would no longer have to drive in fear through their streets, nor would it be a safe haven for insurgents.

The plan was pretty simple. The infantry battalion was going to set up defenses around the town while some of its units entered it and routed out the enemy. When the enemy fled, we would be able to capture them on their retreat. We would do this by setting up multiple vehicle checkpoints and observation posts on the outskirts of Gharma. The main body of the Outlaws was to assist in this defensive perimeter while one of the platoons, White, assisted the assault force within the city. All this would take place in the early morning to catch the insurgents off guard.

Although it didn't promise any combat action, we were all still excited to get a little revenge for not being able to take part in the last attacks. I, for one, was excited and hoped I might be able to use the SMAW this time around. My chances were slim, but there was always hope.

We got word of the mission a couple of days beforehand, so we were able to conduct training for the scenario. The scouts of all the platoons split up into sections to have classes, and the vehicle crews met with Captain Shepard and the rest of the platoon commanders to go over the mission on a terrain model to see how it would be conducted.

The tricky part was the terrain we would be traversing. Al Gharma was a farming town. Unlike farms in the United States, farms in Iraq consisted of many irrigation ditches and canals to supply water to their crops. This created very narrow and difficult terrain, especially for vehicles as large as an LAV. Not only were the roads narrow, but they were made out of dirt. This caused a big problem because with the combination of the weight of the vehicles and the erosion from the canal water sloshing up against the sides of the road, the banks of the river could easily give in and overturn a vehicle. So rehearsals were absolutely necessary, as were the classes.

The day of the mission arrived, and with it came the anxiety and adrenaline that filled the air. Everyone seemed completely revved up and excited to be going on this mission. After a quick briefing of the mission, we conducted vehicle and personnel checks and then loaded up onto our vehicles.

The LAVs started up their engines and began pulling away, one by one, from the parking lot. Any Iraqi who saw the convoy passing by must have had chills going down his or her spine. For a half mile down the road, I could see the train of LAVs heading toward their destination. The amount of firepower in a company of LAVs is tremendous or terrifying, depending on which end you look at. With fourteen LAV-25s, a few LAV

TOW variants and mortar variants, and about fifty infantry scout Marines, the Outlaws were a force to be reckoned with.

We traveled down a series of roads and paths. The night was quiet with very little illumination. This made it hard for the drivers of the vehicles to navigate through the maze of canal roads that led to our destinations because their sights were very limited and the depth perception was horrible.

I was standing on the floor grate in the scout compartment with only my shoulders and above showing (something we learned after many IED patrols and explosions). Lance Corporal Redd was doing the same thing on his side and had his M-249 SAW resting on its bipods on the scout hatch. We had been out for only about thirty minutes when we started to close in on our selected defensive position.

Lance Corporal David Grove was doing a hell of a job negotiating the very narrow, crisscrossing dirt roads that followed the canals. My vehicle commander, Staff Sergeant Phelps and the gunner, one of my good friends, Sergeant Mike Honigsberg, were also helping Grove steer the vehicle when he couldn't see clearly.

I was scanning the sides of the roads and canals, noting the various shacks that were set up alongside the canal. It didn't seem as if the noise of the vehicles was waking anyone up, which was good. I looked over to Redd to make sure everything was going all right on his side. He nodded and gave the thumbs-up, and I returned to scanning.

After a few minutes, I figured we must have been getting close to our position. I let my mind wander for a bit about being home and other random thoughts. They were interrupted briefly by a slight dip in the road. It was common for the vehicle to lean slightly to one side or the other when we were in this type of terrain. I didn't take much notice and went back to scanning some more. But then I noticed something was wrong.

The vehicle was leaning more and more to the right and wasn't straightening itself. Grove was gunning the engine and turning the wheel to try to get the vehicle back on course. But it was too late. The side of the road gave way, and our vehicle took the plunge into the canal.

I was starting to fall inside the vehicle just as the top scout hatch that I was leaning on decided to close itself. It smacked me right on top of the head. Fortunately, I was wearing my Kevlar helmet, but even with that, it knocked me straight down to my knees. Everything inside the vehicle came crashing down on us, and the momentum of the flip had us rolling around and smashing into one another. It reminded me of the cartoons when a character would get inside a barrel and then go tumbling down a hill. We were helpless.

However, luck was with us that night. The portion of the canal that our vehicle flipped into was only about five feet deep. And as luck would have it, the vehicle didn't flip upside down but rather on its right side.

My whole team was confused for a second, and then the adrenaline kicked in. We needed to get out, and we needed to do it fast. Who knew what else could happen to the vehicle, and we weren't about to stick around to find out. I unlocked my rear scout door and tried to open it. The problem was that the back scout doors were designed to open vertically on their hinges, like a typical car door, not horizontally. Since the doors were made out of steel, they weighed nearly two hundred pounds each. Being on the left side of the vehicle and due to the way my body was positioned, it was nearly impossible to push the door upwards. Fortunately, Redd and Zabala had kicked their back door open and, as the vehicle was laying on its right side, the door opened downward. They got out and immediately went about trying to help the remainder of the crew. Doc and I were in a bit more trouble. Water was rushing in, and we couldn't seem to lift the door open long enough for both of us to escape.

Finally, I was able to get the back door open just wide enough to squeeze my legs out and gain some footing on the door that was submerged in the canal, the one which Redd and Zabala had pushed open. I planted my feet firmly on the submerged door, stood up, and with all my might raised the top door. I don't know how I did it, but I figure it was because of the fear of drowning and one hell of an adrenaline rush.

I was able to hold it open long enough for Doc Barajas to slide out, and suddenly the little bit of friction that was helping me stand on the submerged door gave way, and I slid underwater. Unfortunately, my wrist was still in the door frame when the hatch came crashing down. A sharp pain ran through my hand, and I winced and clenched my teeth. Now was not the time to worry about that, I thought. I still needed to make sure everyone else was okay.

Redd and Zabala were half submerged in the water, trying to pull Staff Sergeant Phelps out of his turret. The canal was very narrow when the vehicle fell, and the turret crashed into the other side of the canal, which happened to be the side that our vehicle commander was on. Staff Sergeant Phelps had injured his back in the fall, and his flak jacket was hindering his ability to easily escape through the hatch.

Sergeant Honigsberg slid out of his turret hatch and started to help Redd and Zabala in their efforts to free Staff Sergeant Phelps. That left Grove. Grove was a different story. He was fresh out of LAV school when he came to our company and still had some of his teachings embedded in his head. He did what he was taught to do, something that can be seen as honorable: he went down with his vehicle, and he was going to continue to do so until he could fix the problem because he felt he was to blame.

He started banging on his escape hatch, trying to lift it to get out. I jumped from the road onto the side of the vehicle to help him open the door. He had a handful of documents and gear that he was determined to take with him, as well as his rifle and helmet. Not only that, but he was furious.

I reached out to give him a hand in lifting himself out of the vehicle. He straightened himself out and jumped over to the canal road. I asked him if he was all right, and all he did was look in shock at what had happened to his vehicle.

"Fuck! Fuck! God damn it, I am in so much shit!" An endless stream of foul language spewed from his mouth as he took in the damage that had occurred.

Not only did I notice a bit of anger in him, but there was fear in his eyes. I tried to calm him down and let him know everything was going to be all right.

"Grove, chill out. It's not your fault. Everything's going to be all right," I said calmly, trying my best to make him relax.

"I'm in so much shit Corporal Tanner. I'm gonna get fried for this," he said, shaking his head in disbelief.

Regardless of what I said, he kept shaking me off and cursing at himself. He blamed only himself for what had happened to the vehicle and wouldn't let anyone talk him out of it.

While this was all happening, the rest of the platoon had stopped to set up a defensive perimeter around the accident. Sergeant Learn's vehicle took up rear security, Sergeant Krall's took up forward security, and Lieutenant Snipes brought his vehicle over to our position.

He jumped out of the vehicle and made his way to me. He immediately wanted to know if everyone was all right. I gave him a brief situation report letting him know everything that had happened from my perspective, and I informed him of the state of shock Grove was in. He went over to Grove to give him words of comfort and to let him know that it wasn't his fault nor would anything happen to him. Coming from the platoon commander, it meant a lot to him, and he relaxed a bit.

Lieutenant Snipes surveyed the scene and assessed the damage. Staff Sergeant Phelps was lying on the side of the road with Doc Barajas attending to him. Lieutenant Snipes talked with him a bit to find out more of what happened and to ensure he was all right. He then spoke with the rest of the crew and headed back to his vehicle to send a situation report to the company headquarters.

Meanwhile, all of our equipment and vehicle gear was starting to sink into the bottom of the canal. Gasoline, oil, and a few other chemicals were starting to pour into the water surrounding the vehicle. We had to recover as much of the gear as possible before it was too late. I had Grove, Redd, and Zabala provide security around the vehicle while Honigsberg and I took off our camouflage shirts and jumped into the canal to recover what we could.

The canal water was chilly and smelled horribly of diesel. The chemicals started to coat our bodies and clothing as we took gear out of the water piece by piece. After recovering what we could feel outside of the vehicle, we started to search inside. It was an absolute mess. Mud and water coated everything. Ammunition was strewn about the compartment. Wires were mangled. Our gear was everywhere.

I called for Redd to set up a poncho for us to lay out the gear on so it could air dry. As we waded through the water in the compartment, the chemicals started to burn our skin a little bit. My arms felt as if a thousand needles were poking them, and it seemed as if my crotch was on fire. Honigsberg and I were both joking about how we wouldn't be able to have kids anymore. It took us nearly an hour to recover everything we could possibly find, and it felt like an hour too long. By the time we got out of the water, my whole lower torso was itching and burning, and I was soaked from head to toe. We looked at each other, laughed for a bit, and then carried on with organizing and cleaning the gear.

Lieutenant Snipes was back at the scene and was tending to Staff Sergeant Phelps. We found out that he seriously bruised his lower back when the vehicle flipped over. It probably didn't help too much that everyone was trying to pull him out of the turret in tight quarters. They had laid a blanket over him to keep him warm.

Lieutenant Snipes came over and inspected all the gear we found. All he could do was laugh; there was nothing else he could do because there was no point in being angry. He informed us that a tank recovery vehicle was on its way to try to pull the vehicle out.

When Lieutenant Snipes passed word over the company radio frequency that one of the vehicles had flipped, Captain Shepard reiterated the need for safety and awareness on the terrain we were traveling. However, it didn't seem as if it mattered much because about three hours after we flipped our vehicle, Blue Platoon lost one of their vehicles too. Lance Corporal Daugherty misjudged a turn and drove straight off of it into the canal. Unfortunately for them, the canal was a lot bigger than ours and much deeper. The vehicle sank to the bottom of the canal and almost killed the whole crew. Daughtery was stuck inside his compartment but was fortunate enough to escape at the last minute. All their gear was submerged in the canal, but fortunately, Corporals Amstutz and Afraidofbear were able to recover most of the gear other than Lieutenant Rowell's pistol and a sleeping bag.

The area where our vehicle had flipped was right in front of a few small houses. When sunrise came, a few of the local villagers came out to see what happened. The family whose house we were in front of was a bit amused by the situation but helpful. They brought out shovels to help in creating a ramp in the side of the road to pull the vehicle up on. In return, we gave the children some of the snacks we had from our MREs and watched in delight as they devoured them.

A few of the other villagers were a bit more cautious of us and stood around in the distance staring. Some were even a bit suspicious looking, which made me nervous. We were helpless in our current situation, and if the enemy were to engage us, we would have been slaughtered.

Eventually, the tank recovery vehicle showed up with a few more personnel to provide security and to assist in removing our vehicle from the canal. It was a huge monstrosity with a tow hook on the back. The recovery crew began to operate the tow cable by releasing enough cable to reach our vehicle. They attached the cable to the left side of the vehicle and pulled the cable taut. Once they felt that they were ready to begin pulling, everyone stood far away just in case the cable snapped. The recovery vehicle started to pull. The tank tracks tore into the ground, and we watched as the LAV moved forward. However, the recovery vehicle was pulling as hard as it could with no luck.

We figured that the side of the canal road was too steep and that we needed to make it into more of a slope. So a few of us went to digging a better ramp than the one we had made. Even some of the Iraqi men sitting around wanted to help us out and grabbed a few shovels and jumped in. When we finished, the recovery crew reattached the cables to the vehicle and gave it another try. The vehicle revved its engines again and pulled with all its might, but to no avail. The vehicle made some progress, but it was dragging on the bottom of the canal, which created more resistance and added weight.

We thought we might have to either blow up the vehicle to prohibit the enemy from using it or possibly get it airlifted out, but either option would have kept us exposed for an even longer period of time. Fortunately, someone came up with the idea of reattaching the cables to different points on the vehicle where it would give the recovery vehicle more leverage and stop the LAV from dragging on the bottom of the canal. We crossed our fingers and gave it one more try.

The driver of the recovery vehicle gunned the engine, and the tank tracks once again bit into the dirt. At first, there was no movement and hopes started to drop, but then there was a little bit of progress. It gained some momentum, and the recovery vehicle started moving forward. A few seconds later, our vehicle was back up on the road with water rushing out of the doors and mud smeared everywhere. It was a sight for sore eyes.

The Iraqis started cheering and slapping one another on the back, believing that they had played a key role in its recovery. We thanked them all for helping us and gave a few more MREs to the children. Some of the children began to enter the canal water to grab the floating debris or food that was floating about. Grove began to reassess the damage and see if there was any more gear lying inside the vehicle that was recoverable. I had the rest of my scouts gather up the equipment and load it onto the other vehicles. We loaded Staff Sergeant Phelps into the back of one of the other vehicles so he could rest his back.

The recovery vehicle attached our LAV to its tow hook, and we all piled into the remaining three LAVs. We drove back to base to start the long process of cleaning all of our gear and fixing the vehicle. When we arrived on the base, Blue Platoon's LAV, which had also fallen in, was sitting in the maintenance bay area while its crew was cleaning and organizing the gear they had recovered.

Staff Sergeant Phelps was brought over to the medical building to be checked on. I began to help my crew offload all the wet and dirty gear. I started to pick up a heavy object when I felt a sharp pain travel down my arm. My wrist was throbbing. I had not noticed the pain until we got back to base. I showed it to Doc Barajas, and he brought me over to have it looked at in the medical building. The other corpsmen thought it might have been broken, so I was taken over to Camp Fallujah, where they had doctors examine it and took X-rays. They determined that it wasn't broken. But I might have damaged the muscle a bit around my wrist, so they gave me a splint and told me to lay off of it for a week. That never happened, but I did use the splint.

It took a while to get all the necessary parts to fix our vehicle. Our crew worked as a team to ensure that the vehicle would be up and running as soon as possible. We scrubbed the rust from the gear, cleaned the inside, wiped off all the mud, and helped fix all the broken parts. We continued to work on the vehicle for about a week, with the crewmen doing most of the work. Eventually, a new LAV was brought to our base and became Captain Shepard's vehicle. We were able to take the captain's old vehicle and transfer all of our gear over to it. With the vehicle came the driver, Lance Corporal Pete Rankin. Unfortunately, the rule with the vehicles was that the driver went wherever the vehicle went. So Grove had to go over to Headquarters Platoon until his old vehicle was fixed. In the meantime, he would also act as the driver for the captain's vehicle. We missed Grove and the humor he brought to the platoon, but he was right next door at all times, so he would visit a lot.

In between the time we were working on repairs and acquiring a new vehicle, my scouts and I still went out on patrols from time to time. Eventually, while still waiting for ours to get repaired, we were allowed to take a LAV-L on patrols. Sometimes, if we weren't able to use the "L," I would ride with Sergeant Jones's team and would scatter my scouts among the other vehicles. And then there were times when we didn't even go out with the rest of the platoon, which caused us to miss a few cool missions.

No one was seriously injured, that was the most important thing, A few cuts and bruises, but nothing we couldn't handle. I was extremely fortunate that day, and it reinforced my superstitious habits of rubbing Buddha and talking to the stars. Too bad it didn't always work.

# CHAPTER 19
# VEHICLE BOMB

The initial assault on Fallujah was finally over, and we were allowed to go back to Camp Baharia to clean up and get some chow. Everyone seemed to be happier. We were back to a semi-normal routine of showers, food, internet center, and games. On top of it all, we were all now officially combat veterans with loads of stories to tell and things to brag about.

The company mission went back to the normal routine of vehicle checkpoints and MSR patrols. However, this particular day and this particular patrol would be the first of many to remember.

Third Platoon had gone out on a routine patrol. While on patrol through one of the small towns outside of Fallujah, one of the scouts noticed artillery guns lying on the side of the road with spent artillery shells all around them. Near the artillery pieces, the scouts noticed a couple of Iraqi civilians using torches to cut up the guns into pieces, which they would take back home. It was brought to the attention of the platoon commander, Lieutenant Rowell, who then gave the order to halt the patrol. Lieutenant Rowell directed his scouts to dismount the vehicles and take pictures of the artillery guns and ammunition to send to back to the COC. He had the vehicles pull off to the side of the road and set up a defensive perimeter around the site.

Sergeant Leuba, the scout squad leader, directed his scouts to fan out to survey the area. Leuba had Corporal Afraidofbear take pictures of the guns while Corporal Justin Hall spoke with the Iraqis to figure out what they were trying to do. The platoon sergeant, Staff Sergeant Ron Ducharme, had placed his vehicle at the far end of the site closest to the road. Rather than have his scouts deploy with the rest of the platoon, Ducharme instructed his scouts to stay put and provide vehicle security.

About ten minutes went by with no sign of any car traffic. Little did they realize there had been a car trailing their patrol for quite some time. Afraidofbear was taking pictures of the guns and was wrapping it up while Hall was still talking with the Iraqis. One of the Iraqis said they had permission to cut up the guns and presented a piece of paper to Hall. Still suspicious, Hall went up to one of the guns and tried to open up the breach to see if there was still a round in the gun. The last thing he wanted was one of these guys taking home an artillery shell to use as a future IED. He could hardly budge the hatch open, so another one of Hall's scouts came over and began banging on it with a rock in hopes of prying it open.

Suddenly, the car that had been following them from a distance began to get closer. It seemed as if it was going to continue on a path past the platoon until it made a left onto the street Blue Platoon was near. Staff Sergeant Ducharme made his scouts aware of the situation and told them to stop the vehicle. The scout section leader in the vehicle, Corporal Scott "Vinny"

Vincent, put out his right hand in the stop gesture (showing your left hand is considered rude and offensive). The driver of the vehicle came to a halt by the side to the LAV and started yelling something. Vincent informed Staff Sergeant Ducharme that the driver was trying to say something. Ducharme leaned over slightly in his turret and propped the right side of his helmet off of his head so he could hear what the driver was trying to say.

Those unforgettable words were "Allah Akbar" (God is great).

In the split second it took for the driver to yell those words, the vehicle disintegrated into a ball of flame. A vehicle suicide bomber, our company's worst fear, had come true.

Hall heard the explosion in the distance. For some reason though, it didn't register that it was one of their vehicles. He thought that the artillery shell in the gun had gone off from them banging on it and presumed that he was dead or dying. When he realized that wasn't the case, he turned around and saw Ducharme's vehicle destroyed. The engine block was skidding down the road and shrapnel from the explosion was flying everywhere. One of the Iraqis began screaming in pain because a piece of shrapnel had hit him. Hall took off running back toward Ducharme's vehicle to try to provide any help he could. Unfortunately, it was too late. His good friends Vincent and Wilfong were killed by the blast.

In the meantime, Lieutenant Rowell instructed Botty to get his vehicle into communication range of the company headquarters to begin reporting the incident, request backup, and get a medical evacuation to their location as soon as possible.

That day, at that particular time, as it seemed with almost every horrible incident, our platoon was the react force. It took our platoon about thirty minutes to gear up and get out to the site. When we got there, it was one hell of a sight to see.

Blue Platoon's scouts were in defensive positions around the incident. The destroyed vehicle was still smoldering. There was a deep sadness that filled the air.

Lieutenant Snipes ordered the vehicles to set up a defensive 360 around the scene. He then had all the scouts dismount and take up the defensive positions of Blue Platoon's scouts and halt all vehicles that tried to come within range of the incident. My squad leader, Sergeant Jones, and I met up with Blue Platoon's scout leaders to get a rundown of what happened. We then walked the area to see what damage had been done. I saw one of my buddies, Lance Corporal Paul Valliere, a scout from Third Platoon and a guy I had gone to infantry school with, in the prone position with tears welling up in his eyes. A few others were doing the same. Valliere kept on saying something about another friend of ours, Lance Corporal Thiel, being hurt. He was about to say something else but was called away to load up onto his vehicle. Two other friends I had gone to infantry school with, Lance Corporal Patrick Walsh and Lance Corporal Jason Wheeler, were set up in a defensive perimeter around the scene as well. I could see that they were in disbelief and greatly saddened. It looked as if they didn't know what to think, as if the whole situation was so sudden and forceful that they were shaken and in shock. I tried talking to them and some of the other Third Platoon scouts, but it was as if whatever I said was just a distant echo to them.

Sergeant Jones and I approached the scene of the explosion, and it was shocking, to say the least. The vehicle that had been hit was destroyed. The whole right side was burned and poked full of holes. Pieces of the armor on the left side looked as if they were peeled back like a sardine can. The interior was charred and smoking. The turret was shredded. There were spots of blood running down the turret and the inside wall of the scout compartment. About ten feet away, there was a fifteen-foot-wide by six-foot-deep hole in the ground. Part of the engine of the car was about twenty feet away from the vehicle. The engine block from the LAV was a good hundred feet away. The rest of the car was scattered in pieces along the road for about a hundred yards. Among those pieces were bits of charred human flesh, most likely that of the suicide bomber.

From what we were told, Corporal Vincent, the scout section leader for Third Platoon, and Corporal Joshua Wilfong, one of the combat engineers for the platoon whose other job was a scout, were the ones standing up in the scout compartment at the time of the blast. They were instantly killed by the blast. Staff Sergeant Ducharme was riddled full of shrapnel and his face was completely burned, but fortunately, he lived. Some shrapnel hit the navy corpsman, Doc Ferguson. Lance Corporal Thiel, another friend of mine who had gone to infantry school with me, was missing a piece of his skull. Supposedly, the sight glass, which allows the scout to look outside when sitting down inside, blew inside and slammed into the side of his head, breaking a piece of his skull off. Another scout, Private First Class Williamson, was slightly burned and wounded from some shrapnel too. Fortunately, the gunner and the driver remained relatively unharmed compared to the others. The whole thing was a horrible sight to behold. It took about another hour for a support team from MEF headquarters to come out and clean up the mess.

That was my first experience with death. Up until that point, I had never lost anyone close to me. I'd never attended a funeral or been to a wake, so the experience was completely unfamiliar. I never really knew how I would handle death. But suddenly, I didn't have a choice. Death was going to teach me its lesson whether I wanted to learn or not. I just went completely numb inside. Maybe it was the numbness or just the shock of the incident, but I didn't shed a tear, I just went numb. I never really knew Vincent and Wilfong that well, but I did know they were both good Marines and they were my Outlaw brethren. Others in the company dealt with it a bit differently, especially those who were truly close to the fallen. Sergeant Alfonso Nava, one of my good friends and an engineer attached to our platoon, was close to Wilfong and I could tell he was visibly shaken by the whole thing. There were some days when we were still stateside that you could catch Nava and Wilfong sitting outside the barracks drinking beer, with Wilfong busting out some tunes on his guitar while Nava sat back and enjoyed the music. Sergeant Leuba and some of the other scouts had served in Alpha Company with Vincent, and you could see on their faces that they were deeply hurt. But, for me, I just went numb. I internalized the loss and pushed it to the back of my mind, hoping to forget it forever. I think that was how I have come to deal with death since that day. I keep a special place in my memory for those who are lost, but I refuse to dwell on it for too long because I'm afraid it might hurt too much. However,

Vincent and Wilfong were someone's best friends, brothers, or sons. So for some, that tragic incident will be forever burned in their memory and a constant source of pain.

That was just the beginning of the blood that the Outlaws would shed before we came home. Little did we know we had a lot more coming.

# CHAPTER 20
# OUTLAW MEMORIAL

Since the first deaths in the Outlaws, the song "Taps" has had a new meaning to me. As a new Marine, I just thought of it as an old traditional song that was played at the end of the day on base. I had heard it in movies, but it never held any meaning. Now, every time I hear it, it brings tears to my eyes because it means so much. In fact, I hope they play Taps when I am laid to rest.

The week that Vincent and Wilfong passed away, twelve other Marines died too. The battalion that we were attached to held a memorial service for their fallen Marines, and ours were included. For something put together in the middle of the desert with little resources, it was a nicely held service.

We were all brought out to the front of the camp chapel. In total, there were about three hundred Marines, each in his individual company formation. In front of the formation were the battle memorials dedicated to those fallen Marines. A rifle with a bayonet attached stood vertically atop the desert boots, with the helmet over the stock of the rifle and the dog tags of the fallen hanging from the handle or trigger guard. They were lined up side by side in perfect alignment.

Standing at attention, in a column to the side of the formation, was one friend of each fallen Marine. Sergeant Alfonso Nava was in the formation to say farewell to Wilfong, and Sergeant Leuba was there for Vincent. The small detachment began marching toward the memorials until they came to a halt in front of their respective comrades.

The battalion commander said a few words, as did the chaplain. "Taps" was played, and each Marine placed a second pair of dog tags around his friend's rifle and completed the ceremony with a farewell salute.

When the detachment completed their farewells, they moved off to the sidelines, and the rest of the battalion, along with our company, formed a line and walked past each Marine's memorial. When a Marine approached the first memorial, he saluted and held his salute until he passed the last memorial. It was a very touching event.

After the ceremony was over, we were allowed to approach individual memorials and say whatever last words we wanted to say. Some took pictures. I stood by each one, said a few last words, and then walked away, hoping no more would have to die.

A couple days later, a few Marines and Sailors had a great idea. They were going to erect a permanent memorial for the Outlaws' fallen Marines. They built a wooden cross and stood it up on a slab of concrete in front of the base chapel. On the stand for the cross, they placed squares of marble to cover the base. On two of the marble tiles were the names of Vincent and Wilfong, with their birth and death dates and their platoon. A flag rested up against the cross, a couple of nonalcoholic beer cans were placed on each side of the memorial, and a few other tokens of remembrance were placed there. Someone painted a colorful drawing of an angel on a piece of plywood and stood it up behind the memorial. Everyone from the Outlaws would go over to the memorial from time to time to wish them and their families well or maybe just have a few words with them. For the next month, every night, someone would go out and light two candles next to the cross in memory of them. The family bond was beginning to grow; unfortunately, it took two lives to do so.

Throughout our deployment, that memorial would continue to grow with the names of the fallen. Sadly, six more names would be added to the base—six brothers; six sons; six fathers; six Outlaws who will never be forgotten.

All of the ceremonies we had and the Outlaw memorial will forever be embedded in my mind, and I will never forget my friends. I hope they rest in peace wherever they may be.

# CHAPTER 21
## SCOUT

A few days passed before the sorrow from the loss of Vincent and Wilfong lifted. Life had returned to normal, and patrols had resumed as usual. Improvised explosive devices were becoming almost an everyday event; however, we were lucky enough not to have any more casualties, just a bunch of close calls.

Our days were split into three shifts. Eight hours for missions, eight hours as the react force, and eight hours of downtime. Most of the time, my platoon's missions and patrols ended up being conducted at night. We considered our shift the worst because we went on our missions at approximately 8:00 p.m. and came back at 4:00 a.m. It wouldn't have been so bad if we had air conditioning in our tents; however, when we came back from patrols, we would only have about three hours of sleep before the morning sun became too hot.

On one of these night patrols, I met one of my greatest and most-missed Iraqi friends. It was around 9:30 p.m., and our platoon was already out on another routine patrol to safeguard the MSR and ASRs. We had received a report that there was gunfire heard near a local mechanic's garage, so we were told to go investigate. The scouts loaded up into the vehicles, and we took off to our destination.

We arrived about five minutes later. There was not a soul to be seen and an eerie silence surrounded the area. The scouts deployed from the vehicles to patrol the surrounding area and check for anything unusual. After patrolling and determining it was secure, I ordered my section to set up a small defensive perimeter near the shop. The area we were near was on a small mound on the left side of the shop overlooking Fallujah. From time to time, I could see a red or green tracer shoot into the sky above Fallujah. Once in a while, a parachute flare would be launched, which gave the sky an eerie glow.

Suddenly, the sound of dogs barking erupted from the right side of the mechanic's shop. Around the corner came three little puppies that seemed to be some kind of Labrador-German Shepherd mix, the cutest little things ever. Sadly, they looked so malnourished; I could see their rib cages poking through their skin.

When they noticed me, they started barking even louder. This was a problem because it would give away our position to anyone nearby. So I stared the three of them down and shushed them which calmed them a bit; however, they wouldn't come any closer to me. I reached into my patrol pack and took out an MRE. After rummaging through it for a few seconds, I pulled out a beef stick. I tore a piece off of it and placed it in the palm of my hand. Slowly, I extended my arm and opened my hand to invite them to come a bit closer. Only one of them budged, the smallest of the group.

Scout, which I came to call him later, edged closer and closer. His siblings followed suit but trailed a bit farther behind. Cautiously, Scout reached my hand

and began eating from it. I tore a few more pieces for his siblings and gave it to them. They were a bit more reluctant to eat from my hand, so I had to lay the food in the dirt. They were ravenous. I went back into my MRE to find some more food and fed them all a little bit more. Once the three little rascals finished eating what little I had, two of them began to tussle a little bit. Scout, however, followed me around wherever I went.

I decided to crawl up onto the edge of the small embankment next to the shop to get a better view of the city. I put my NVGs on to see what was in my immediate surroundings. When I took the NVGs off of my head a minute later, Scout was sitting right next to me scanning the horizon. It was almost as if he were mimicking me, trying to be an actual scout himself.

His siblings ran over the hill and started wrestling a bit on the other side, but Scout stayed where he was. He looked over to me as if to say, "Give me an order." I looked back to the city, and so did he. This continued for the remainder of our time there. While I was sitting there scanning the area, I was trying to figure out how I could take this puppy back to base with me. If it had been closer to the end of the patrol, I may have been able to do it, but we still had another six hours to go and I couldn't hide him in the back of the vehicle for that long.

Eventually, we got the call "Scouts in!" from my vehicle commander, Staff Sergeant Phelps. I stood up, made sure my scouts heard the command, and then ran back to the vehicle to load up to go somewhere else. Scout came running after me, wanting to load up into the vehicle. He had the saddest eyes and such a questioning look, as if he were saying, "Why are you abandoning me? Please take me with you." It tore my heart.

Our vehicle began to move and kick up dirt.

"See ya later little guy. Stay safe out here," I whispered as we began to move away. Scout and his siblings chased us for a bit, barking the whole time. The image of Scout staring me down as we took off is etched into my memories.

I don't think I ever saw him again, and sometimes I wonder what might have happened to him. I truly hope he found a home and someone to feed him. I have seen what insurgents use animal carcasses for, and I hope he wasn't one of them.

That night was one of my fondest memories of Iraq. After the patrol, I told myself that when I got home, the first thing I wanted to do was to get a dog and train him to be just like Scout.

# CHAPTER 22
# DAILY ROUTINE

The way our shifts were usually set up was that we would patrol for eight hours, be the react force for another eight, and have off for the last eight. Some days were ordinary, and others were broken up with new missions or happenings. But almost every day, we would try to find what little there was to do on base to entertain us.

Our days always seemed to start off the same. Most of our shifts either began at 8:00 p.m. or 2:00 a.m., two of the worst shifts to have because either way we barely got any sleep.

Each morning at 2:00 a.m., the guard on watch would come into our section of the hooch with a flashlight and wake the platoon. We usually had thirty minutes to get ready for the mission. In thirty minutes, we had to shit, shower, and shave, and then prepare our vehicles and gear for the mission. Once that was all done, the platoon commander would come out and give us our mission briefing. It was normally the same each day, but sometimes they would give us a cool one to do.

Once the briefing was over, we would load up on our vehicles and take off. Normally, we would patrol the main service route (ranked the most deadly in Iraq at the time) back and forth, which was about fifteen miles in length. We would break it up by stopping and setting up hasty listening and observation posts for about thirty minutes, and then we would go back to patrolling again. At times it could get extremely boring, and at other times it would be full of action.

Eventually, we began to devise new ways to break up the monotony and keep alert. A few people in the platoon had a lot of knowledge about the LAV and the small tweaks that could be made for added comfort. One of the most common add-ons in many of the vehicles was MP3 players hooked up to the vehicle intercom. This was probably one of the coolest features that we concocted. We would go on patrols, and the music would play in the background. The crew was able to hear it at all times, and whoever was wearing the CVC helmet in the scout compartment could hear it too; however, we usually hooked up the squawk box (speaker) in the back so all the scouts could hear. I had made it a point to bring my MP3 player with me on the deployment, and it held up well in the desert. Any player would do; the one we used for our vehicle was my Creative Zen. I loaded it up with over a thousand songs so we would never run out of new things to listen to. It lasted nearly the whole deployment, but on one patrol it fell underneath the turret and broke. Having music on patrols was something we sorely needed. Although some might view it as interference, it actually helped in keeping us awake and alert, and it kept morale high.

One of the worst things about our usual shift was that it ended when the heat was starting to get bad. We would usually return from patrols around ten in the morning, clean our weapons and vehicle, and then lie down for a nap. Unfortunately, we didn't have working air conditioning until July, and trying to fall asleep in 100 to 120 degree weather is damn near impossible. The solution was to strip down to our boxers. I would lie there and start to feel the sweat drip down my face. Within thirty minutes, my pillow would be soaked and it looked as if I had wet my bed. It was insane. So after about an hour of trying to fall asleep, I would get up to go find something to occupy my time. This was where things would get interesting.

Initially, Camp Baharia had little to offer. The only thing that provided some form of entertainment was the internet center. It had phones and computers for e-mailing and surfing the internet, but one could only do so much of that before getting bored. We needed other things, things that brought hours of fun. Seven months away from civilization made us very innovative.

*****

Spades was the ultimate pastime activity for us. It was equivalent to playing pool and drinking beer, except in our case, we sat down, played cards, and drank our Cokes. The game developed teamwork and friendships where there were none. Depending on who I played against, it would be for fun or would involve some cash.

There were several high-profile spades partners who were the ones to beat, but the most infamous were Sergeant Joseph Clarkson and Corporal Jermaine Whitley, two of the shadiest spades players in all of spades history. The rules stated that there was no talking, something they never did, but I swear they developed some form of signals to let each other know what to do. They were almost unbeatable and were probably the only two people in the military to come out of Iraq for the better, money-wise. Gunny Rossignol and First Sergeant Sprague were another force to be reckoned with, as were Lieutenant Rowell and Lieutenant Nunnally. These guys were the honest ones who played it straight. They lost, but it was a rare sight.

Clarkson was usually the one to set up spades tournaments. Some involved cash, and others were for reputation. They would draw about ten to fifteen teams, and more often than not, he and Whitley would win.

For one of these particular tournaments, I decided I wanted to enter, and I wanted to be able to put the deadly duo in their place; however, I didn't have a partner I was confident enough to play with. After a few practice games and a bit of searching, I found the best spades partner whom I believed could help me accomplish my goal, Sergeant Alfonso Nava. Nava and I played for a few hours a day to get to the point where we believed we could win the tournament. He and I clicked in that we knew, to an extent, what the other had—but somehow Clarkson and Whitley knew exactly what each other had, so Nava and I had to one-up them. We devised a plan that was sure to win.

We sat down one day and came up with hand signals that would alert the other about what to throw next. One might consider it cheating, but someone needed to put them straight and beat them at their own game.

"All right Nava, I think I've come up with a pretty solid plan," I said with an evil grin on my face.

"What's that?" he asked.

"So here's the deal," I continued. "When we hold our cards in our hand, we'll use our fingers to signal what we want the other to play. Holding your cards with one finger means you want me to play a spade, two fingers a club, three fingers a heart, and four fingers a diamond."

"Cool. What about numbers though?"

"That's the easy part. After you raise the amount of fingers for the type of card you want me to play, then just tap those fingers against the cards the amount of times to tell me what number to play. Ace will be one and it will go all the way up to thirteen for a king. Pretty easy, right?" I asked, my grin getting wider as I congratulated myself for coming up with such a great plan.

"Dude, I like it!" Nava exclaimed. "We should definitely do a few practice rounds before we sign up for the tournament as a team."

For the next few days, Nava and I played a few rounds with other groups of guys to test out our new hand signals. We perfected our signals and how to display them without giving ourselves away. Every game we played, we won without exception. We had become a bona fide threat to the Clarkson-Whitely duo.

When the day of the tournament came, Nava and I blew through the competition. Each team we went up against, we easily defeated. But with each win, we still didn't feel like we were champions. We needed to test our plan against Clarkson and Whitely.

We finally got that opportunity a few rounds later. We were in the semi-finals of the tournament and our opponent happened to be our self-appointed archenemies, Clarkson and Whitley. The match was a best two out of three and we were determined to sweep the series.

The first round of the series started off well. Nava and I stuck to our plan and used the hand signals we perfected. Clarkson and Whitley were none the wiser. While we played, I was trying to figure out what they did for hand signals. From what I could gather, it seemed like they were doing a mixture of signals using their hands as well as the words they used. I tried calling them out on it numerous times but they kept denying it so I let it be. After about twenty minutes of playing, Nava and I soundly defeated them.

We went into the next round overly confident of our skills. I'm not sure if they caught on to our signals but it felt like they might have because they quickly defeated us with little effort.

It was tied one to one and we went into the final round of the series. The stakes were high and both teams knew it. Nava and I took a quick break to gather our wits and discuss strategy. After five minutes, we headed back to the table determined to win. For the next few minutes, it seemed like no team had a clear advantage. And then, it seemed as if a light bulb went off inside. Clarkson and Whitely clicked and began to methodically beat us down until they won the final round.

We left the tournament defeated. We were so confident in our plan but it appeared they were better prepared. We may not have defeated them that time, but on occasion we would play small games and beat them, making a few dollars on the side. The best part was seeing their faces whenever they did lose.

*****

Iraq is home to many creatures and insects, but the one that tops the cake has to be the camel spider. I'm sure many people have seen the picture of someone holding up a camel spider that is attached to another one, supposedly mating or something of the sort. Their size varies from a few centimeters to a few inches, and they aren't the prettiest little things either. Although they look dangerous, they weren't very harmful. Despite the rumors, they are not poisonous, nor do they eat camels. I think the worst they can do is eat small rodents and lizards. The greatest thing about them was that some of the guys were deathly afraid of spiders—which made them all the more useful.

Corporal Klinger, a good friend of mine, was one of these Marines. He was from Texas, loved his job, and was friendly and knowledgeable in his field, but he was a common prankster. On occasion, we would hear Klinger laughing about something he had done to someone that he found funny. He even got me a few times, too, but he had a weakness. Klinger had a severe case of arachnophobia, and it gradually became worse as the size of the spiders increased. Some brave souls would try to catch the spiders and let them loose near Klinger or even toss one toward him. To see a combat-hardened Marine scream like a girl was probably one of the funniest things I had ever seen. Hell, even I have done it sometimes, but seeing it done to one of the platoon's pranksters made it all the better.

The other type of arachnid we would come across on base was the scorpion, the most common being a small black scorpion. I have no idea if they were poisonous, but there were no reported bites or symptoms, so I doubt they were very harmful. The entertainment came when we decided to create fighting matches.

Right outside of our hooch was a small pit that had a bunch of trash thrown in it. Occasionally, we could look down into the pit and see scorpions skittering about and the occasional camel spider looking for cover. One day, out of pure boredom, one of the Marines from another platoon found a camel spider, put him in a box, and named him Jimbo. He was about two inches long and brown, with something that looked like fur covering his body. Jimbo wasn't the biggest camel spider I had seen but was fearsome enough to get some shrieks out of Klinger. Someone got the brilliant idea to jump into the pit and capture a scorpion to hold a fight match. The Marine jumped down with a container, kicked some rocks and trash around, found the scorpion, grabbed him by his tail, and threw him in a jar. In the few minutes we knew him, we decided to call him JimBob. He was about an inch long and black, with a muscular tail and a ferocious-looking stinger.

Someone acquired a cardboard box, and the fight began. Both insects were thrown into the box and went into their corners. Everyone was betting on the camel spider to win. From the rumors everyone believed, we thought the spider would devour the scorpion in one fell swoop. Never underestimate the underdog.

The spider started to cautiously inch toward the middle of the box. It didn't seem as if he was interested in fighting; rather, it looked as if he was trying to find a way out of the box. The scorpion moved with lightning fast speed. Fearing the spider might be trying to attack, he swiftly attacked the spider with his tail, barraging him with a dozen stings before the spider quickly backed away. Jimbo was frightened and was intently looking for a way out. He ran along the walls searching for some kind of opening. Jimbob saw the vulnerability and attacked again, cornering the spider and hitting him with several more stings. Jimbo seemed to be slowing down as if he was hurt or dying. Jimbob sensed the death walk and decided to back off. I think he believed the spider was dead.

As everyone's hopes of seeing Jimbo eat Jimbob started to fade, the fight became less interesting. After we saw Jimbob decimate Jimbo, we decided to let them both loose to go back to their business. Jimbob vanished underneath the flooring of our hooch, and it seemed as if Jimbo was going to pass away in the sand. However, once Jimbob disappeared, Jimbo gathered himself up and took off for cover.

The fight brought us about ten minutes of entertainment, probably some of the best entertainment we experienced.

*****

Even with all the crazy and unusual stuff we found to do, there was still a lack of entertainment, which probably accounted for the great amount of ingenuity. If we couldn't find something to do, we made it.

At first glance, the lake within Camp Baharia seemed useless. There was a lot of talk about filling it up to its maximum capacity and allowing the Marines stationed there to swim in it, but it never came to fruition. But some people did find other uses for it. A couple of Marines from our company and the infantry battalion stationed there created makeshift fishing rods. They would stand by the side of the lake, put a piece of food from an MRE or the chow hall on the hook, and throw it in, hoping for something good. Believe it or not, there were bass in there, some measuring around two feet long. Eventually, Marines like Sergeant Madden and Lance Corporal Afraidofbear wrote home asking for someone to send out a real fishing rod. Their fishing rods weren't expensive; they looked like something a child would use, but they got the job done. They never caught anything of significance but at least it brought some of the comforts of home to Iraq. Unfortunately, fishing came to an end shortly after it started when the base sergeant major decided it was inappropriate.

*****

Sports were another pastime that brought camaraderie. The company brought a few recreational items to Iraq, and the most popular was football. For physical training in the morning, some guys would play football. It became so popular that we would have platoons challenge each other. There was even a tournament that was set up, and Second Platoon ended up winning it all.

When football got old, we had soccer and softball. Lance Corporal Duarte and a few other soccer fanatics set up a makeshift soccer goal and would play for hours outside, showing off their moves. It never got big within the company, but there was a decent-size following. Softball became more popular as time went on. We brought a few bats, balls, and a bunch of gloves with us.

This was a game we could play at any given time during the day because we didn't exert too much energy. The parking lot became our playing field, and the walls and concertina wires were the boundaries. The platoons would set up batting lineups and field positions, and we would play for hours until everyone got completely bored.

\*\*\*\*\*

Finally, there were video games and board games that helped kill time. Around May, the 2/1 Marines set up a decent-size tent that stored the game and movie room. They had several Xbox, PlayStations, and GameCubes set up with a variety of different games. The movie room had a few couches and chairs scattered about. Every night they played a different movie, and during the day movies were available upon request.

A board game that was popular among a few of my friends and me was Axis and Allies. Sprenger had asked a family member to send it out to him, and when he received it, a few people came forward admitting that they were avid fans. The most common four players were Sprenger, Lieutenant Nunnally, Sergeant Madden and I. Sprenger and I would usually be the Allies, and Madden and Lieutenant Nunnally loved to be the Axis. We would set up the game in the officers' housing or the COC and would play through the night hoping that one side would come out victorious. Of all the games we played, we never did get to finish a full game due to patrols and other interruptions.

*****

There were moments, however, when there wasn't much to do. This was when I would go to sleep, write a letter home, visit the internet center, or go to the chow hall. The chow hall was never something to brag about, though.

At the beginning of the deployment, the food was horrible. We received t-rats or MREs, the building itself was extremely hot, and there was nothing to drink but water. But I must admit that around summertime, it got a lot better. Camp Fallujah began making enough food for both camps, so 2/1 would send over their chow-hall Marines to bring the food back to our camp and supply us with better food for breakfast, lunch, and dinner. If we were lucky, they would also bring soda and ice cream with them, too. With the help of the Gator, Gunny Rossignol was eventually able to set up a makeshift chow hall in our little encampment so we didn't need to travel as far to eat. Admittedly, our luxuries started to increase toward the end of the deployment.

*****

After our downtime was over, we either had to go back on patrol, or we were on react force. React force wasn't really that bad; however, we had to be ready to react to any situation at a moment's notice, so we needed to be within five hundred meters of the tents at all times. Depending on what our platoon commander had in mind for us, we were either allowed to use the eight hours for leisure, or we would have training classes in various subjects to keep our minds sharp. The classes varied anywhere from basic weapons classes to raids and patrols. Sometimes we would set up small simulations to act out particular missions. Other times we would try to develop more efficient and effective SOPs (standard operating procedures) for our platoon. Whatever we did, it ended up just a way to waste time.

The end of the day would come, and with it came the evening (or whatever part of the day you considered evening) rituals. Dinner would come and go just as the other meals, and we would continue on with whatever we were doing. Some people would take showers, but never every day. In the beginning I took showers about once every two weeks because we only had one shower; however, when we acquired a shower trailer, I took one as often as I could, which was about every other day.

After we took showers, it was usually around the 10:00 p.m., which was when the heat would go down to bearable. This was about the only time of the day we could get a decent night's sleep. I would roll out my poncho liner and isomat on my cot and lie down, dirty or clean, and sleep for about four hours before I had to get up to do the same thing over again.

*****

There were some things other than leisure time activities that gave some variations to the day. Almost every day, like clockwork, we would come under mortar and rocket attack. The first few times, it was scary as hell. We could never hear the mortars being fired, but as they came closer to their target, they made an eerie whistling noise like that of a Nerf football. Everyone would run like chickens without heads toward bunkers to take cover. But once we got used to it, we would stand in place and wait for the attack to stop. Luckily, nothing bad ever happened, but there were a few close calls. The one area the insurgents lacked in most was aim. Our tents were huge, towering over our base wall by at least twenty feet. Therefore, I believe it right to say that they couldn't hit the broad side of a barn.

The other thing that broke up the monotony was the IEDs. I think we averaged about two to three a week that would explode on our patrol or that we found. Sometimes there was no damage, sometimes there was a lot. So in essence, we were all gambling. Each day was a new day to play Russian roulette with our lives. We woke up each morning wondering if it was our turn. This was pretty much what our life was like for seven long grueling months.

# CHAPTER 23
# CLOSE CALL

After about two months' experience dealing with IEDs, we had become fairly familiar with the bombs and what they may be hidden in. However, we never stopped learning.

On one of our usual patrols along the same route and about the same time (not many people must have passed the terrorism awareness MCI), we were lucky enough to spot one. Corporal Klinger was the gunner of Lieutenant Snipes's vehicle. He was standing up in the turret assisting Lieutenant Snipes in the IED scans. We were going to go over an overpass to go back in the direction we came from when Klinger flinched. He called over to the lieutenant that he had spotted an IED as they passed it, hoping to stop the patrol before the next vehicle passed it in case it was detonated. It just so happened that the next vehicle was mine.

The first two vehicles continued forward for about two hundred yards, and Sergeant Learn's vehicle stayed behind about two hundred yards. Our vehicle was positioned about a hundred yards from the bomb when we came to a halt. Staff Sergeant Phelps called over the intercom for me to take someone with me to go over and check it out to see if it was actually a bomb or just trash.

I rogered up, got out of the scout compartment, and pulled out my binoculars to get a better glance of what I was going to get close to. From what I could tell, it looked like an old inner tube. However, Klinger had stated he saw a wire sticking out of it, which I could not confirm with my binoculars, so I had to get a closer look.

I called for my saw gunner, Lance Corporal Redd, to provide security for me as I checked the area. I went through the normal procedures of scanning the immediate area of the bomb looking for any signs of wire leading to the bomb and then scanned the area two hundred yards out looking for a possible triggerman. After determining it was clear, I decided we could get closer to get a better look, but I was hesitant. I scanned my surroundings again, as did Redd, to see if I could spot any triggerman in the distance. The last thing we needed was to get close and then blown to bits.

We inched closer to get a better look, and I noticed a thin copper wire protruding from the tire. I called back that I did see the wire, but I couldn't determine if there was any explosive inside. Redd walked up to it and gave it a nudge with his boot. I flinched and looked at Redd as if to say, "What the fuck did you do that for?" As it didn't explode, I leaned over and gently opened the split inner tube to glance inside.

"Holy shit! Get back, Redd. IED!" I yelled.

We slowly inched away from it, and when we were about twenty feet away, we took off like bolts of lightning.

When we got back to the vehicle, I informed Staff Sergeant Phelps of what I had seen. It seemed to be some sort of artillery shell. He passed the information back to

Lieutenant Snipes, who then gave a call to EOD (Explosive Ordinance Disposal). Lieutenant Snipes needed some more information on it, though. He wanted to know if there was anything attached to the shell that would act as a triggering device. I had no idea because I didn't care to see past the shell to find out more. However, we needed to find out, so he sent Sergeant Nava out to assist me.

As we approached the IED, I informed Nava of what I had done and seen. He then proceeded to do the same thing. He slowly opened the tube to peer inside. After identifying the shell, he couldn't find any triggering device, but he wanted to check out the other side of the tube to make sure. He opened the other side wide enough to see a box that contained what appeared to be the electronic board of a remote control car with wires connecting it to the artillery shell. All the triggerman needed was the remote control to detonate the bomb.

"Shit, Tanner, it's an IED," Nava said in a worried voice. "Let's slowly back away and act like it's nothing big just in case someone is watching us."

We cautiously backed away from the explosive and jogged back to our respective vehicles. By this point, we figured if there was a triggerman, he would have pulled the trigger, so we were a bit more relaxed.

Eventually, a team of EOD specialists arrived at the scene. Lieutenant Snipes went over to inform them of the situation and called Nava and me over to give a better description of the IED. Meanwhile, some of the other members from EOD were setting up a computer and putting a robot on the road.

The robot was interesting looking. It looked as if it were straight out of television, with an long arm protruding from its body and four all-terrain wheels. Mounted on top was a camera that acted as the "eyes" for the robot. The computer was more of a laptop with a joystick. It controlled the robot wirelessly and had an image on the screen of what the robot saw.

The EOD team began to direct the robot toward the bomb. Once it made it to the IED, the camera zoomed in on it to give the controllers a better look. They guided the robot to grab the inner tube with its arm to look inside. The camera showed the box with the innards to a remote control car and the wire connecting it to the bomb. Carefully, they ordered the robot to extend its arm toward the wire to pull it. I could feel the apprehension in the air. It seemed as if everyone was holding his breath while the robot was pulling the wire. What seemed like hours took mere seconds to perform. The robot pulled the wire out, and nothing happened. The controllers then directed the robot to grab the remote control box and wire and drag it out from the tube.

Once they were certain that the bomb couldn't be detonated, an EOD staff sergeant donned a bomb suit. How it protected against bombs, I will never know. It looked like a giant space suit but a bit boxier. The most it looked like it could do was protect against burns.

The staff sergeant cautiously approached the inner tube. He opened up one end of it and slid the artillery shell out. The shell was huge. We later found out it was a South African 155 mm artillery shell, which is a longer version of an American artillery shell. He hoisted the shell onto his shoulder and began to walk back to us.

When he was about halfway back, he lost his footing and fell backward. Everyone leaped for cover. I closed my eyes and hid behind the Humvee. I was anticipating a huge explosion. Nothing.

The staff sergeant stood back up, waved his hand to tell us he was OK, threw the artillery shell back on his shoulder, and walked back toward us. I think my stomach was still in my throat when he got back. He had a big grin on his face and apologized for scaring the crap out of everyone. Everybody had a good laugh about it, but inside I could tell everyone was just thanking his lucky stars that it didn't go off. Some probably wanted to smack the guy upside the head.

That IED was one of the first ones we actually found intact. Most of the others just blew up. We were extremely lucky this time. If there had been a triggerman watching us, I wouldn't be telling this story. I'd be lying in a box in pieces.

# CHAPTER 24
# INCOMING

On one particular hot May night, our platoon had just come back from a patrol. It was around 2:00 a.m., and most of us had already fallen asleep. I was in a deep sleep, which I sorely needed since I wasn't getting much. I knew it was a good sleep because I was dreaming, which I hardly ever did out there.

*I was back in the United States having a big, juicy steak at the dinner table with my family. We were all talking about how we were doing and current events. I was trying to talk my dad into accepting the idea of me getting a motorcycle. My mom was just giving me a look as if to say, "You're crazy."*

The dream slowly faded away. Another picture popped into my head. Jets were flying overhead, but I couldn't see them, I could only hear them.

Swoosh!

Swoosh!

Swoosh!

There was lots of commotion. I stirred from my sleep to discover that the noises weren't a dream but reality. I didn't realize what was going on until I saw a streak of light glow through the tent ceiling and then heard an explosion in the near distance. Our base had come under attack by a huge missile barrage. People were rolling off their beds. Some were trying to throw their flak jackets and helmets on and were searching for their rifles. Some were already running out of the door with their gear on backward. Others tripped in all the disorder and were getting trampled on. It was utter mayhem. As I look back at it, it must have looked somewhat amusing: thirty-two men with nothing but their boxers on, grabbing their rifles, tossing their flaks and helmets on hurriedly, running for the door and screaming for everyone else to get out.

I rolled out of my bed and hit the wooden floor with a thump. My breathing started to escalate. Everyone was running for the bomb shelter outside. However, since everyone was trying to get to the same place, they were causing a pileup. So I lay on the floor, grabbed my flak jacket and helmet, and covered my upper torso with it. I looked over and saw a few others do the same. It was pointless to try to run at this point.

As suddenly as it came, it stopped. I listened for a few more seconds and then slowly rose from the floor. A few others stood up and followed me out of the tent to the bomb shelter. It was possible that another barrage would soon follow so we wanted to be better protected. I walked outside to see everyone huddled in both bunkers. But it wasn't only my platoon; all the other platoons were hanging out in the other bunkers.

Of course, as Marines like to do, everyone made fun of one another. We were teasing each other about who ran faster, who was the most scared, who didn't put his stuff on the right way, or who might have pissed his pants. It was actually quite a funny sight and humorous once it was all said and done.

After it was determined that the coast was clear, we surveyed the damage. None of our living quarters or equipment were damaged. The missiles had landed a little farther out, some hitting open areas of land about fifty yards away and some going into the lake. The only thing that was damaged was a port-a-john on 2/1's side of the base. A missile had actually struck it and blew it to pieces. Shit was everywhere—literally. I believe the total count was about forty-two missiles that had landed within the walls of Camp Baharia.

I went back to bed that night happy that I still had my life and no one got hurt. However, my heart was racing, and I was still a bit on edge. That had to be one of the scariest nights I ever had.

After that night, I made sure that my gear was more accessible. Mortars continued to bombard the base almost daily. None ever came as close, but a few did cause some inconveniences, such as our gravity shower getting blown up. But we became used to it, and some guys were actually able to determine whether the mortars would even come close to hitting us. I became so accustomed to it that I wouldn't run to the bunker until after the first one hit the ground, and then I would run like hell if it was close.

To this day, I am still a bit affected by loud noises and sounds that sound like missiles and mortars. It was funny to see me on my first Fourth of July back home. People must have thought I was nuts.

# CHAPTER 25
# GATOR

Who said you could never bring toys to combat? In all the madness and mayhem, the one thing we needed was a toy to bring us a little fun and excitement. That toy ended up being a Gator.

White Platoon was out on a regular patrol doing the usual IED, counter-mortar, and counter-rocket missions when something came up. A supply convoy had been hit, and they needed some support while they cleaned the mess up. The vehicle that had taken the brunt of the explosion was a trailer carrying John Deere Gators to one of the camps nearby. Somehow, some way, White Platoon was able to acquire one of the Gators in return for their assistance. As fortune would have it, the supply convoy was hit about two miles outside of base, so the trek back to Camp Baharia wasn't too bad. Lieutenant Nunnally had two of his scouts drive the Gator back; one was for security while the other drove. If you could have only seen it: two big, bad-ass Marines armed to the teeth driving around in a tiny, quad-style golf cart. Hilarious.

I was sitting on my cot watching a movie when I heard a bit of commotion from outside. It sounded as if someone had a dirt bike and was having one hell of a time with it. A few of us stepped outside the hooch and saw Gunny Rossignol zipping back and forth across the dirt parking lot, throwing in a few donuts from time to time. To see a man who had been in the Marine Corps for sixteen years as a hardcore infantryman doing donuts on a golf-cart-looking vehicle was comical. To add to the amusement, First Sergeant Sprague came out and jumped in the passenger seat. They switched off driving and were doing all sorts of tricks, spitting up sand as they went. The two of them were like kids in a toy store.

That was when it all started. There were over one hundred men and only one toy to play with among them. They had to make a logbook for the Gator so we could sign up to use it at a designated time. Everyone in the company wanted to use the Gator for some task or another—go get food from the chow hall, go to the small PX on base, help with the sandbag-working parties, and about anything else that you could possibly think of. And of course we didn't drive it responsibly. We drove it as if we would never see it again. One would think we were constantly racing an imaginary opponent.

Although we goofed around on it a lot, it did bring some sorely needed assistance. It had a flatbed on the back, which allowed us to use it to transport items. Towards the end of the deployment, Gunny would send someone down to the base chow hall to pick up our portion of food for each meal. No matter what anyone was doing, when we heard the Gator come zooming up to our area around chow time, we would drop what we were doing and line up to get some food. It was such a privilege to have chow delivered to us rather than walk a half mile to get it, especially after a long day of work and patrols.

Another big use was for working parties, sandbag

and ammo in particular. Before the Gator, we had to have the whole company line up and pass the ammo or sandbags down the line to reach its destination. This could take hours sometimes and wasted a lot of manpower that could be used elsewhere. The Gator could take on a heavy load and transport it anywhere in a matter of seconds.

However, we abused the poor thing. We would add so much weight to it that it would run like an overburdened mule. By the end of our deployment, it barely ran. We had no more spare tires, it made weird noises, the alignment was off, and it didn't run as fast as it used to. Gunny wanted to try to load it into one of our containers to bring back to the States, but it wasn't worth it. After we handed it over to our relief, Alpha Company, it was on its last legs. It probably didn't run for much longer.

To this day, it will forever be remembered as the trusty workhorse and backbone of the Outlaws. BEST. TOY. EVER.

# CHAPTER 26
# EXPLOSION

The IED, counter-mortar, and counter-rocket patrols were almost always the same, but sometimes something unexpected would happen. Most of the time, the unexpected was never wanted because it usually meant casualties.

On one such patrol, our platoon was conducting IED patrols about midway between Camp Baharia and Abu Ghraib. Sometimes we would do the sweep on the main road, but on occasion we would conduct them on the ASRs (alternate service route). I always felt safer doing them on the ASRs because I felt as if the insurgents didn't think we would travel them very often. Never, ever underestimate the enemy.

I was standing in my usual position in the scout compartment, and Lance Corporal Redd was doing the same. We were driving on an ASR in a column formation with about fifty meters between each vehicle. To the right of us were farms with fresh vegetation, irrigation ditches, and water reservoirs scattered about the land. In the far distance were a few houses that most likely belonged to the farmers, with a long dirt road coming up to them from the main service road.

I was scanning the area surrounding our vehicle when Sergeant Honigsberg passed over the internal radio that he had noticed a suspicious car parked on the side of the main road about five hundred meters ahead of us. He said he noticed three men in the vehicle who were watching us as we drove along the route. We kept a closer eye on the vehicle as we continued forward along the ASR.

BOOOOOOOOOOM!

My knees buckled from under me as I dropped inside the scout compartment. Smoke enveloped our vehicle, and our vehicle came to an abrupt halt. My ears were ringing uncontrollably, and I could feel a liquid rolling down my ears. I was scanning the inside of the vehicle to make sure everyone was OK and to see if I had lost any limbs. Everything seemed so hazy and distant.

"Scouts out, scouts out!" Staff Sergeant Phelps was yelling.

Everything happened so fast that I was still trying to gather my thoughts when we were ordered to get out and secure the area. With all the training we had received on IEDs, nothing prepared me for my first close-up encounter with one. I was still in a state of shock and checking myself for wounds. Physically I was fine, but everything sounded so distant, and there was an uncontrollable ringing in my ears. I was disoriented and confused for a short time, but then I started to come back to reality. I turned to Redd and saw that he was shaken but all right. Doc was asking if we were both all right and then started yelling to Honigsberg and Staff Sergeant Phelps to ensure they weren't wounded.

I jumped out of the back door and got my scouts in a small, hasty defense around the vehicle. I looked for the car that had been on the side of the road, but it had vanished. About ten feet behind us was a giant hole in the dirt road where the IED had been. I looked up at Staff Sergeant Phelps and saw him holding his hand. Some shrapnel or debris must have been kicked up and scratched the backside of his hand. Fortunately, he was fine, and Doc eventually patched him up.

How we managed to go through that blast unscathed is still a mystery. I believe I have a vague idea of what transpired. The three men in the car were probably the triggermen. They were sitting on the side of the road trying to figure out the time interval between each vehicle. After the first two vehicles in our platoon passed the IED, they had a pretty good idea of when to detonate the explosive. When our LAV passed over the location of the IED, they triggered the device, and it exploded as planned. However, we had a couple of things in our favor. The triggermen must have been extremely nervous, and their timing was slightly off, which explained why we passed the IED by five feet before it exploded. Additionally, they must have placed the IED incorrectly. After I looked at the hole where the explosion occurred, it seemed as if they had buried the explosive too deep. Not only that, but it was placed on the side of the road instead of the middle, where it could have done more harm. So the bomb was unable to achieve maximum damage because the dirt road absorbed most of the explosion and kicked up debris and smoke. We learned two lessons: our good fortune was amazing, and even though the enemy may have missed, they were getting better.

Although we had a pretty good idea who the triggermen were, Lieutenant Snipes decided we should cover all possibilities and search the surrounding area. He had the scout teams meet at my vehicle, and then we proceeded to make our way toward the farmhouses. We fanned out across the farmland in a skirmishers formation to cover the most area. The terrain was rough, which made traversing it rather difficult.

The incessant ringing in my ears wouldn't stop as we made our way toward the houses. Everything sounded as if it were distant and echoing. I brought my hand up to my head to wipe away the clear liquid oozing from my ears. I shook my head in hopes of regaining my normal hearing, but it was all for naught. Great, I thought, I'm never going to hear right again.

Sergeant Jones called me over to tell me what we were going to do. He wanted all of our teams to surround the two houses in a defensive perimeter. He then wanted me to talk with the occupants of both houses to find out if they knew anything of the explosion or had seen anyone in the area.

We reached the houses moments later and had the scouts surround both buildings. Sergeant Jones and I went to the house on the far left and approached what appeared to be the eldest man of the house. He seemed very friendly and said he knew nothing of what happened, but he believed he saw men run off in the distance right after the explosion. His whole family started to gather outside and talk to us. They seemed like a very friendly group and tried to offer any help they could. After determining we couldn't gather too much more information from him, Sergeant Jones called back to Lieutenant Snipes to inform him what we learned.

Lieutenant Snipes sent the information back to company headquarters, and they relayed a message back stating that they were going to send out an actual translator to speak with the residents. I informed the man and his family that they would need to stay put while we waited for the translator. The man was very obliging and tried to accommodate us in any way he could. He offered us food and water, but we respectfully declined.

I decided to walk over to the other home to see if I could gather any additional information from the occupants. According to the man from the first house, the second house was occupied by his distant relatives of some sort. I approached the house with Redd, Zabala, and Doc by my side. I knocked on the door, and a middle-aged man opened the door. I had Redd and Zabala secure our immediate area while I tried to converse with the Iraqi. I told him of our situation and asked if he had seen anybody. He said pretty much the same thing the elderly man did. Since I couldn't get much more out of him, I informed him that a translator was coming to talk with him soon. He was as courteous as the other man and tried to accommodate us. Again we declined and just stood around waiting.

I tried to make small talk with the man and asked him about his family and what he thought of Americans and other random things. From what I could make out, he told me that the Americans were definitely a help and that the insurgents were very bothersome. He told me that the insurgents were threatening families to cooperate with them and hide explosives and weapons for them. If they didn't help them, they would kill them and their families. The whole situation sounded so horrid, and I suddenly felt awful for them. Here we were in the United States taking everything for granted, and these people were worrying about how to make a living and stay alive in the process.

He continued to speak to me, but his voice sounded as if it were fading away. I started to get tunnel vision and could feel my legs turning into Jell-O. What must have happened was that after the explosion, adrenaline was pumping through my veins, and once I calmed down, the rush subsided and left me weak and dehydrated.

The man started asking me if I was all right. He indicated that my face was turning pale and offered me some water. I declined it and grabbed for my camelback (water pouch) tube to take a sip of water. I sucked, but nothing came up. I must have drunk it all while we were patrolling and never got to refill it. The man offered the water to me again, and I hesitantly accepted it. He walked inside and came back out with a large metal bowl filled with water and handed it to me.

I grabbed the bowl and looked at it to inspect what I was about to swallow. The bowl was unusually cold, as if it had been taken out of a refrigerator. The water looked relatively clear with the exception of a few bits of something floating around inside. It didn't matter; I needed the water desperately, or I would pass out. I took a large gulp and started to feel the life flow back through my body. I thanked the man many times and handed the water over to my scouts. Each of them took a long swig of water and passed it on to the next, making sure to thank the man for his generosity. When it was empty, I handed him back the bowl and thanked him immensely. He could see that we were pleased, which put a huge smile on his face.

After we had been waiting about a half hour, the interpreter and his small entourage showed up to question both men. The interpreter came to my area first and questioned the man. He basically got out of him what I had found out. Meanwhile, since the interpreter's team had taken over our small area, I brought my team over to Sergeant Jones's position to find out what was going on over there.

As we approached, I could hear Jones saying something to the family, and they in turn were trying as much as possible to say something back in English. When I finally got close enough to see what was going on, I couldn't help but chuckle. A few of the scouts were providing security around the building. Sergeant Jones and a group of scouts were sitting in the shade with the Iraqi family drinking what looked like Kool-Aid and tea. Son of a gun, I thought. Here I am sweating my ass off and declining nearly every offer of desperately needed water, and the rest of the scouts are having a picnic with a nice Iraqi family. All I could do was shake my head and smile.

Sergeant Jones had the scouts switch out with each other to have a little bit of Kool-Aid and tea while we waited for the interpreter to come over to our position. While we waited, the Iraqi family tried extremely hard to be good hosts by offering food and shelter and trying to make small talk. For a moment, even though everything around us was hell, it felt as if nothing was wrong and we were doing training back in the States. I felt so comfortable for that small amount of time.

In time, the interpreter came over to the house and began the process of interrogating the family. After about twenty minutes of talking to everyone, he gathered the same information that we had already found out. He wrote down everything he had learned in his notepad and told us we could head back to the vehicles.

As we all started to get back into our team and begin our walk back to the vehicles, the families of both houses gathered around and waved good-bye. We thanked them again for their kind hospitality, shook their hands, and went on our way.

I remember crossing back over the farmland and thinking how there was still a little bit of sanity left in this insane world.

# CHAPTER 27
# COPS & ROBBERS

There were very few times that something exciting and entertaining happened on a routine patrol. However, when something did pop up, we made sure we made the most of it.

It was a normal night patrol on the MSR. We had been traveling the road back and forth for a few hours. During that time, we received information over the radio that there was a car traveling the MSR that would fire at convoys as it passed them. They sent the description of the vehicle over the radio along with a license plate number. Three men armed with automatic weapons were traveling in a white Mercedes-type car. The license plate was in Arabic, so there was no point in writing it down because it would take forever for us to try and match it. Now that we had the information, we just needed to find them.

Every half hour or so, we would pull off the side of the road and set up a hasty listening/observation post (LP/OP). We would stay there for about twenty to thirty minutes and then resume our MSR patrols. This routine carried on for the better half of the patrol.

About three hours before our shift was up, we pulled off the road to get into yet another LP/OP. Five minutes after we got into our positions, one of the gunners noticed a vehicle and a truck that was parked on the shoulder of the far side of the road. After a closer look, they noticed it looked similar to the car we were looking for. Not only that, but men were standing to the side of the car and looked as if they were digging or possibly dropping something on the ground. Instantly, we thought we had caught insurgents in the act of planting an IED.

Lieutenant Snipes had all the scouts run over to the car's position while the LAVs surrounded the vehicles and blocked traffic. Sergeant Jones took his section of scouts and searched the car while I took my section to search the truck. I had the driver stand by his vehicle as I searched him for weapons. Lance Corporal Duarte and his team searched the truck. We came up empty-handed on the truck, so I began to question the driver. All I could gather was that he stopped by the side of the road to fix something, and then the car pulled up in front of him. He sounded pretty innocent, but there was still something out of place.

Sergeant Jones's discovery was a different story. He relayed the license plate description back to MEF headquarters, and it came up a match. He immediately began searching the three men but couldn't find anything. Slightly disheartened, he had his team go through the car. That was where the treasure lay: three AK-47s, a pistol, a hand grenade, and a few hundred rounds of ammunition. In addition to that, they found a box with wires that could have been used to create some kind of remote detonating device.

He immediately put the three men on the ground and zip tied their hands behind their backs. His team searched the car more thoroughly but found nothing else. After receiving the description of what had been found over the radio, Lieutenant Snipes decided to have the truck driver zip tied too. Meanwhile, I had a few scouts search the area where we believed they had been digging and found nothing, raising suspicions even higher. But with the language barrier and limited interrogation skills, we couldn't figure out anything else.

With nothing left to find, we now had to figure out what to do with the vehicles. We couldn't just leave them on the side of the road because they would either get stolen or be used to make car bombs. So we did what we thought was best and brought them with us to Camp Fallujah.

The truck was a giant, orange eight-wheeled truck. It was stick shift, but not of the type that I had driven in the States. The car was an oddity. It was an old Mercedes model with a few upgrades on the inside. The radio had some kind of navigation device built in to it. After fiddling with the controls for a bit, I couldn't even figure out how to turn it on. I could open it and close it, but nothing else seemed to work, which bothered me to no end. It had been a long time since I had listened to a car radio, and I wanted the damn thing to work.

Since I didn't know how to drive the truck, Lieutenant Snipes had Duarte drive it and assigned one of the scouts to ride with him as security. I jumped in the Mercedes with Forsyth to provide communication with the platoon just in case anything happened. I was ecstatic. Nothing could have sounded so great at that time. I got to drive a Mercedes in Iraq. How many people would be able to say that?

We integrated the vehicles into the middle of the platoon to provide added security. I started up the engine and waited for the word to move out. Once Duarte indicated he was ready, we started our trek back toward Camp Fallujah to turn in the prisoners and vehicles.

The drive back was one of the most memorable rides I have ever had. Forsyth and I continued to mess with the radio in hopes that it would turn on. I pushed the seat back to give myself some more room and got the feeling that I was riding in style. We were having the time of our lives and enjoying every second of it. We were on a joy ride in Iraq.

When we arrived at Camp Fallujah, we were directed toward the temporary prison building. It was a place where they held prisoners before sending them over to Abu Ghraib. We parked our vehicles outside and waited as Lieutenant Snipes went inside to talk to the guards. I reclined my car seat and relaxed for a bit. After a while, I went over to Sergeant Krall's vehicle to brag to the other scouts how great it felt to drive. Some of the guys went over to the car to check it out and see if they could get the radio working.

We waited for what seemed like an hour. Lieutenant Snipes exited the building, but he didn't seem happy. He called us all over to his location to receive a quick briefing. Snipes informed us that they would not take the three men or the vehicles. Yet the truck driver, the man who was least guilty, would stay at the temporary prison while they sorted his identity out. The only thing they would do was take the weapons, tag them, and give a receipt to the men so they could pick them up in the morning.

"You have got to be kidding me," I said. What the hell was going on? We had just captured the men they had told us to find, and now they wanted to release them. Something was amiss.

"Listen, I didn't make the rules," Lieutenant Snipes said. "We're being told that we have to actually catch them in the act of planting a bomb or shooting at us in order for them to go to jail."

"Ain't that some bullshit," someone behind me said.

Another one of the guys asked, "Sir, we found a cache of weapons on them. What more do they need?"

Lieutenant Snipes seemed just as pissed but knew he had to follow orders. "I know you're all pissed. I am, too. But, orders are orders and we gotta let them go. Let's mount up and we'll drive them back to where we found them."

Some of the guys could be heard muttering obscenities under their breath and complaining about how the whole situation was bullshit as they walked back to their vehicles. Where was the justice in this law system? The only way we could arrest someone was if we caught him in the act and had proof? It made no sense. No one in his right mind would wait to take a snapshot of a crime in progress before apprehending the suspects. However, we were the low men on the totem pole, we had no say.

Once everyone got into their vehicles, Forsyth and I got into the Mercedes, and Duarte and a scout jumped into the truck. We headed out of Camp Fallujah pissed off and a bit demoralized, but we still got a bit of revenge.

Instead of driving the men back to their original spot, Lieutenant Snipes wanted to drive out to a remote area and let them find their way back. We drove off the road onto a dirt path and followed it for about one kilometer. I stopped the vehicle about one hundred meters to the front of the platoon. We got out of the car and brought the Iraqis over to our position. Forsyth and I knelt them down beside the vehicle, and I began to cut their zip ties. Rage rushed through my head, and I wanted nothing more than to hit each one of them on the back side of the head with my rifle. They were criminals intent on killing as many Marines as they could; they knew it and we knew it, but we could do nothing to stop them. They would most likely come back another day and take an American's life, and it would be our fault.

While I was cutting them loose, Forsyth went around the car and slashed each of the tires. Maybe we couldn't do anything to them, but we could to their car. With a broken car, they would have to walk back, giving them time to reflect on the bad things they had done. Justice was partially served in our eyes.

We headed back to the LAVs to load up and return to Camp Baharia. We left that day one pissed-off platoon. It showed us how things actually worked out there. The justice system was flawed. We played by the rules, and they used the rules against us. Something was not right there.

# CHAPTER 28
# COMMUNICATION

I would have to say that the most important thing that was needed to successfully complete our mission in Iraq was not our training, weapons, or LAVs; instead, it was the mail, e-mail, and phone calls. These forms of communication were the tools we needed to keep morale high and get us through the day. It was our key to the outside world.

Mail, a.k.a. snail mail, was probably the least-used but most-wanted method to stay in touch with our friends, family, and loved ones. There were a couple of problems with it, though. Letters and packages took at least two weeks to get to us from the States. Care packages with food in them were susceptible to the heat and being crushed, ruining some of the snacks inside.

There was also the danger of its being blown up on the ride to our base. There was one instance that got our blood boiling. The mail usually came at around the same time every day. Headquarters Platoon would send a couple of Humvees over to Camp Fallujah to bring Captain Shepard to his meetings with the higher-ups and to pick up supplies and the mail that was waiting for us.

On one particular day, when the small entourage came back from their daily run, Sergeant Jibson was empty handed. We were furious and wanted to know why there wasn't anything. He informed us that on the way up to Camp Fallujah, one of the mail trucks had been hit by an IED, and the mail inside was destroyed. How dare the insurgents mess with our mail! The anger radiating from everyone was felt in the air and could be seen as each platoon went out on their daily patrol. We wanted to get revenge; we wanted to show what happened when they messed with our mail. Unfortunately, or fortunately for them, we never found anyone to pick a fight with, and the anger level subsided over the next few days. It never happened again, so I am guessing the insurgents realized that it might not have been a good idea to hit mail trucks.

The beauty of regular mail was the sense of connection with the writer. It felt more personal. Some guys would get mail that was sprayed with their loved one's perfume or body spray. They would walk around the hooch and let everyone get a whiff and be envious. The other great thing was the care packages. If someone ever wants to do something for the troops and make their day, send them a care package loaded with food and magazines. It's the ultimate gift and something that will be put to good use. My family would send me some of the best care packages loaded with beef jerky, candy, Pringles, and magazines. In addition, they had friends who would send me packages too. One church from Brooklyn sent over one hundred boxes filled with an assortment of snacks and treats that I handed out to my whole company. Some company must have thought we didn't wash our clothes, so they sent us fifty boxes filled with boxes of Tide. Gunny Zenoni, Weapons Platoon Sergeant, had his father send us out T-shirts from Miller Light with our company name on it and a cool design on the back. The items we received were all greatly appreciated and sorely needed.

E-mail and the internet were the next greatest things. When we first arrived at Baharia, the internet center wasn't set up, so we could only get in touch with everyone via snail mail. After the initial assault on Fallujah, it was up and running, with two rooms devoted to the computers and one set up for satellite phones. It was our savior and brought much joy with it. However, it had its drawbacks.

The biggest problem was that it was shut down from time to time. If the battalion was going on a major mission, they would shut down the center so no one could pass the information on to his family. It wasn't that they were worried that families would give us away, but if insurgents were smart enough to be able to intercept an e-mail with important material, they could seriously put a damper on a mission. Also, when a Marine or Sailor passed away, they would keep it closed until the family was notified by the military; they didn't want the family to hear it from an outside source. The least common reason was someone getting caught sending vital information. There was only one instance of this, and because of it, they shut the whole center down for a week. Some guy from the infantry battalion we were sharing the base with had sent information to his family about the mission they were about to go on, the time they were going and details of the route—probably not the brightest thing to do.

Even with all the setbacks and closings, it was still our place of gathering. At any given time during the day, I would see a bunch of Marines lined up outside chatting away, waiting for their turn to use a computer.

Sometimes it would take up to an hour just to get a turn. After the higher-ups noticed the popularity of the center, they began imposing time limits on how long a Marine could be on it—twenty minutes. When they realized the time limit didn't stop the huge lines, they decided to make it open for about eighteen hours a day. I would usually go there in the early morning right after a patrol or in the late evening to avoid "rush hour" traffic.

In my opinion, one of the greatest improvements they made was to section off an area for game play. They loaded twelve computers up with the video game Counter Strike and designated one of the rooms just for that. It was a game we could play against each other in tournaments. We would wait in line for hours just to get thirty minutes of game time. Some of us would go inside to watch the others play, coach them, or figure out their game style to beat them when it was our turn. It was our very own arcade room and a great place for friendships.

The phones were a little less popular but a great privilege nonetheless. On my first deployment overseas, we had phones on the ship; however, the wait time was ridiculous, and it cost almost two dollars per minute. People would go broke calling home for thirty minutes. We were a bit more fortunate in Iraq. A company that dealt with the military had set up satellite phones for us that cost only five cents a minute, a drastic change from the two dollars we expected. There were six of the phones in the internet center, and we had special codes to use them. The codes were linked to an account with the company that set up the phones. Whenever we ran out of minutes, we could go on the internet and refill them. After a few months being deployed, the platoon commanders decided that we were allowed to use their handheld satellite phones at certain times of the day. This was an amazing benefit because it allowed us to save time standing in long lines at the internet center; however, we only got about ten minutes to call compared to twenty minutes at the internet center.

The only drawbacks to the phones were the wait time to use them and the delay time in speaking. Since the voice had to travel thousands of miles back home via satellite, there was a delay in talking, which was annoying at first but something we got used to. We couldn't speak at the same time as the person we called, or it would get all jumbled. We had to wait about five seconds before our voice reached the recipient and then another five for the response to come back. Sometimes the satellites wouldn't be working, so the call would just cut off and waste valuable call time. However, the phones were a blessing and a much-needed amenity.

All of these communication devices were what kept us mentally alive and well in Iraq. They provided good news and bad. They helped us along when we were down and brought smiles to our faces when we needed it the most. Without them, I don't know what we would have done or how well we would have completed our missions.

# CHAPTER 29
# THE BOND

I can never say I was a lifer nor that I had tons of experience in the Marine Corps, but I was pretty good at picking up patterns. On my first deployment overseas, the first two months sucked. Marines were taken from their stateside lives and thrown into a squad bay with thirty other Marines whom they woke up to every morning. There was no disconnecting from your work life and relaxing when you got home. Home life was work life, and that was where the problem lay. So for the first two months, everyone had to adjust to this new way of life, and tempers had to settle down before it became a more relaxed atmosphere. The last month of the deployment was slightly difficult as well because everyone was itching to get home, and sometimes tempers flared back up and the atmosphere could become a bit tense. On that deployment, I thought this cycle had more to do with everyone being stuck on a ship than anything else. But lo and behold, the same held true for this deployment, although the adjustment times were slightly less.

There's no particular date that I can pinpoint when the tense period ended, nor is there a particular event that occurred that made everyone transition from adjustment mode to brotherhood. Instead, several factors came into play that I believe made us become the brotherhood that I, and other Outlaws, called family.

*****

The event that began the bond, and one that we all wish we could take back, was the passing of Vincent and Wilfong. Up until that day in April, our company had never sustained any significant casualties, and when Vincent and Wilfong passed, it really hit home that we were in a war zone and that our fellow Marines were getting killed. Their passing felt as if a piece of our soul had been ripped out, never to return. But because of it, we began to grow stronger as a company. I noticed a difference in attitudes. It was as if everyone was getting along a bit better because you never knew if it was going to be the last time you saw that guy. You never want something as tragic as death to bring you closer, but it has a funny way of doing that.

*****

The day of the services for Vincent and Wilfong was another step in the direction of bonding. That day many people passed away, and their lives were honored during the ceremony. It was a very emotional day.

Shortly after the services, I headed back to the hooch. My platoon was scheduled for a patrol later that night and I needed some shut-eye, but a few Outlaws headed over to the chow hall on the other side of Camp Baharia. We shared the chow hall with the 2/1 Marines on Camp Baharia, so the makeshift chow hall was mainly packed with 2/1 Marines, and occasionally you could see a small group of Outlaws at their own table. Due to the recent deaths, tensions were high, and you could feel it in the air.

The Outlaws who went over to the chow hall for a bite to eat had just sat down to enjoy a meal. Corporal Tony Russell, an Outlaw TOW Gunner from Weapons Platoon, was just about to sit down when he overheard a few Marines from 2/1 talking about the recent deaths.

"It's about time they finally had some of their own get killed," one of the 2/1 Marines said.

Big mistake. The last person you wanted to overhear those words being uttered was Russell. Russell was a big, muscular guy with a chip on his shoulder. He was a damn good Marine, but it seemed he was always ready for a fight, regardless of rank. If you disrespected him or anyone he was close to, be prepared to fight, and when you did, you had to fight as if you may not see tomorrow because with Russell, you may not.

"What the fuck did you say?" Russell asked angrily as he turned around to face the Marine. "Did I hear you just say you're glad that one of my brothers passed away because that's what I think I just fuckin' heard."

"Mind your own business," the Marine responded.

"No, I'm not gonna mind my own damn business. You just disrespected one of my brothers," Russell said as he moved forward and got in the Marine's face.

It seemed as if the situation was about to get heated so the guy's buddies stood up to protect their comrade. Instantly, the Outlaws who were sitting at the table with Russell stood up. It was about to be an all-out brawl.

"Everyone calm the fuck down," a staff sergeant from 2/1 said. "Marine," he said in Russell's direction, "you got a problem?"

"Yeah Staff Sergeant," Russell said, trying to calm down and collect himself. "Your Marine there just said he was glad to hear a couple of our Marines were killed."

"I don't give a fuck what he said, you don't come into my chow hall and try starting a fight with one of my guys. You understand Marine?" the staff sergeant said.

"Aye, aye Staff Sergeant," Russell sarcastically said.

Furious, Russell and the guys grabbed their chow and headed back to our side of the camp. The minute they got back to the hooches, you could hear Russell's baritone voice calling out to all the other Outlaws to gather up and head over to the chow hall as one giant force. He was itching for one hell of a fight. He came into our portion of the hooch and explained what had just gone down, and we all got up, threw on our cammies, and were ready to follow him back.

Somehow, Gunny Rossignol and First Sergeant Sprague overheard the commotion and came over to investigate. Someone informed them of what had happened at the chow hall, and you could visibly see the anger on their face. However, as the company first sergeant and gunny, their responsibility was to ensure order and discipline. The last thing they needed was a conflict between fellow Marines when we all shared a common enemy right outside our walls. So Sprague,

Rossignol, Russell, and a few other Marines headed over to 2/1's side of base to discuss the matter with their sergeant major.

Shortly thereafter, the situation was defused; however, there was a lasting impact among the Outlaws. When Russell and the other Outlaws who were over at the chow hall came back to gather us up, no one questioned him. It was as if we all understood the gravity of the situation, and it was our mission to protect the honor and integrity of our brothers, both fallen and alive. We became one mind, one unit instantaneously. It was truly a moment to remember and one that helped us to grow together not only as a company but as a family.

\*\*\*\*\*

In my opinion, the one factor that weighed the most in the Outlaws becoming so close was that we had a fantastic senior staff.

First Lieutenant Earlie Walker, a short guy with a thick Southern drawl, was the company executive officer. Typically, whenever Shepard would give him an order to relay to the company, Walker would interpret it and disseminate the important information to the company and leave out the bullshit. You wouldn't know it from the looks of him, with a stern face and serious demeanor, but he had one hell of a good sense of humor. He treated us like men and was always there to back us when the situation warranted.

First Sergeant Michael Sprague, a brawny guy from West Virginia who came over from the Air Wing to lead our company, was inspiring. He was always the first to lead the way, and he did so with a level head. He, along with Walker, would sift through the bullshit that Shepard handed them and disseminate the useful information to the Marines. He also had a way with words. He wouldn't be the first to admit it, but he really knew how to talk to the Marines. There were times when he would come out after Shepard had given a speech that he had copied from *Lord of the Rings* or *Independence Day*, and Sprague would follow up with a speech that would bring even the strongest men to tears. Sprague was like one of us. He interacted with nearly all of us on a daily basis. He would treat us all like his sons, always looking out for us and caring for our needs. He would get in on spades games and hang out in the hooch and watch movies with us. He was definitely the best company first sergeant a Marine could ask for.

And then there was Gunnery Sergeant Rossignol. Gunny was a medium-build guy who reminded me of the salty gunnies you see in the movies, a guy who looked as if he had gone to hell and back and brought back the devil's pecker as proof. At one point in his career, he was a drill instructor, and you could hear it in his raspy voice, one that probably made quite a few recruits pee their pants back in the day. Yet behind that hard exterior was a truly good man. He treated everyone as equals, regardless of rank. He knew everyone's name, knew a lot of their background, and would go out of his way to ensure they were taken care of. He always had your back, whether you did right or wrong, and would stick with you until the end. And he wasn't afraid to go toe to toe with anyone, even upper brass. Most importantly, he was like a father figure to a lot of us and a friend to everyone. There wasn't a minute in the day that you didn't see him out there helping with sandbags, playing video games, or getting his hands dirty with the other Marines. Gunny was someone you looked up to as a role model.

And last but not least, we had some excellent platoon leaders. There's no way our company would have become so close knit if it weren't for the likes of First Lieutenants David Snipes and Kevin Knox Nunnally and Second Lieutenants Ron Rowell and Bob May. Each was unique in his own way. Each had his own style of leadership. But they shared one common aspect, which was that they were truly good, inspiring leaders. They, like the rest of the senior staff, treated us like men, not as subordinates, and they spoke to us as such. They truly did care for our welfare and had our safety as their number-one priority. You really couldn't have asked for better leadership.

I don't know how it all happened to come together so well. It's hard to find a First Sergeant like Sprague or a Gunny like Rossignol or a platoon leader like First Lieutenant Snipes, but to find a group of Marines in leadership such as these guys and to be able to have them all in the same company leading Marines into combat is a stroke of luck. I'm not trying to take away from the fine staff NCOs or remaining Marines in the company, but there is no way I tell this story with a different set of leaders in place. There is no way the bond we formed would have become so strong. There is no way I would so fondly remember my family, the Outlaws.

# CHAPTER 30
# BOREDOM

It seems crazy to say it, but there were times when I would become absolutely bored out of my mind. During patrols, my mind had to be constantly active. Every little bit of my surrounding I had to be aware of. I never knew what lay around the next corner or what surprise may be hidden beneath a rock. I had to scan each and every individual I encountered and quickly assess whether this person posed a threat to me and the rest of my platoon. I would try to memorize patrol routes and keep a mental picture of the surrounding environment so the next day, when we covered the same route, if I noticed anything different, I could instantly determine if it was something to be concerned about. This daily routine kept my brain hyperactive, which was a good thing because I never wanted to become complacent. However, the moment I was able to let my guard down, which usually occurred back at the FOB (forward operating base – Camp Baharia), my brain became like mush, and I'm sure I can say the same for the rest of the Outlaws. Needless to say, when our brains turned to mush and we were able to relax, that was when the boredom set in. And the last thing anyone wants to do is let a Marine get bored. This was most likely why, when we had downtime, the leadership would try to keep us busy with training classes and maintenance schedules. But there was no way they could keep us occupied every second of the day, and that was when stupid things would happen.

*****

One of the dumbest things I ever did as an individual—because I did a ton of stupid things when I was with a group of buddies—actually happened on a patrol. On this particular day when my stupidity was at an all-time high, our mission was to simply do IED sweeps along several routes. After a couple of hours of doing these patrols, we set up a defensive perimeter a few hundred meters from the nearest road. Once we came to a rest, Staff Sergeant Phelps had my team and me set up a defensive perimeter around the vehicle. I ensured all my scouts were good to go, and then I began to settle into a defensive spot of my own. In the meantime, Lance Corporal Peter Rankin, our new driver, began doing a quick survey of the vehicle to ensure everything was properly running, and Sergeant Mike Honigsberg, the gunner, started scanning the surroundings.

After a few minutes, I started to feel myself get slightly bored staring at a never-ending landscape of sand, so I reached into my pocket and pulled out a cigarette, something that had become more of a habit than an addiction. I pulled out a matchbook from one of the MREs I had eaten, ripped out a match, and quickly struck it against the pack to light it up. A couple of puffs and my cigarette began to ease my nerves. I threw the match to the ground and watched as it fell. That was when I noticed these little black pellets sprinkled in the sand around me. I looked a bit farther out, and the black pellets seemed to be everywhere, surrounding our whole position. Not sure what it was, I picked one up and studied it closely.

This was when I should have started to actually use my brain and not let the curious idiot out of the box. Too late, though. I figured I would try a few science experiments with it. I pulled out another match, lit it up, put the small pellet on the ground, and put the match next to it. Instantaneously, the pellet ignited in a bright white flash, and just as soon as it had lit up, it disappeared. That was fuckin' cool, I thought. I then realized I had stumbled on a whole lot of gunpowder. And again, rather than decide to call it in, I had to light up some more pellets. It helped kill the boredom, which was all I was concerned about at that time. So I began to walk around and collect a whole bunch of pellets, and I stacked them up into a little pile in front of me. When I was satisfied the small mound of gunpowder was big enough, I lit up another match and threw it onto the pile. It let off a hot, bright light for a bit longer this time, nearly singeing my face, and then went out. I figured I needed to do it just one more time for shits and giggles. So I put together a slightly larger pile and threw yet another match on it. Big mistake.

The pile went up in flames, but this time, the flame spread to the other pellets on the ground. "Holy shit!" I yelled to no one in particular. The other scouts looked back at my position in amazement. Staff Sergeant Phelps and Rankin looked over and saw the flame heading toward the vehicle. Phelps, in a state of shock, immediately yelled out to Rankin and ordered him to start the vehicle and move out of the way. He then told us all to get in the vehicle as fast as possible. We all took off as fast as we could toward the back of the vehicle, Rankin fired up the engine, and the second we closed our scout hatches, he gunned it and took our vehicle a good two hundred meters away from the flame. I could swear that flame burned for a good minute before it finally died out.

After we settled into our new position, Phelps turned to me and asked what happened. Knowing I'd be in a heap of trouble, I just told him I had thrown my cigarette on the ground and the gunpowder happened to go off. He bought it, or at least I think he did, because it was never mentioned again. Redd, Zabala, Doc Barajas, and I sure did get a kick out of it, though. We had a good long laugh about it. Needless to say, I never did that again. Instead, there were plenty of other stupid things I would come up with.

*****

No one will ever admit it, but folks used to send care packages full of alcohol to us all the time. And it wasn't just a couple of guys who received these generous packages, everyone was pretty much guilty. And I'm fairly certain this is a widespread occurrence that happens throughout all the services. Some people might question why we would possibly need alcohol in the middle of a danger zone. It's simple. It helps relax the mind in a very tense environment. Imagine being hyper vigilant for seven straight months without a break. Having a little bit of alcohol helped ease that tension and gave us a quick break from the craziness that surrounded us.

During my stay out there, two kind individuals happened to send me some alcohol, and I was more than happy to share it with my fellow Outlaws. One package contained some vodka. It was ingeniously hidden in an empty shampoo bottle. The moment I opened up the bottle, I could smell the vodka. So I stashed the bottle under my cot, prepared to share it with a few of my buddies at a later time. However, the next day I received another package that contained a bottle of Crown Royal. I was one lucky guy. I quickly hid the bottle in with some of my clothes and stashed it under my cot. I needed to wait for the right moment to enjoy it with a few friends.

After hiding the bottles away, I told a couple of my buddies about my little fortune. Sprenger, my best buddy who happened to sleep in the cot next to me, seemed to be just as excited as I. I also let Sergeant Nava, another good friend, in on the situation. We quickly came up with a plan. Our platoon began to do the mid afternoon-to-late-night shifts. We figured that the following night, after our shift was over, we'd all stay up a bit later and enjoy a few sips of the Royale. Once we had a plan in place, I was anxious for the day to come. I told a couple of the other Marines in our platoon about it and invited them to join us. I also decided that I wanted to give the bottle of vodka away. Lance Corporal Doug Raymer, one of my scouts at the time, graciously accepted my offer and took the bottle off my hands.

The night of celebration finally came, and we were all eager to let off a little steam. Once most everyone laid down for the night, a group of about five or six of us headed outside the hooch, brought our camping chairs with us, and set up shop right outside. It was daring of us to do it out in the open, but we weren't overly concerned because it was pitch black out, and we planned on having only a few sips.

When we had all settled down, I slowly pulled the bottle of Royale out of its cover and popped it open. I took a quick sip and passed it on to the guy next to me. As that first sip entered my mouth, I could feel my taste buds scream in enjoyment. It felt amazing to have just a little bit of alcohol for the first time in several months. A few minutes had gone by and we had all taken our fair share of sips. At this point, we all began to feel a slight buzz, and we let go of our inhibitions. One of the guys said we should just keep going and enjoy ourselves. So naturally, I did what anyone else would have done: I took another swig and passed it around. We must have been at this for a good half hour before the bottle went dry. That whole time we were cracking jokes, laughing our asses off, and telling stories of the good ol' times back in the States. As stupid as it was for us to get buzzed, it was probably one of the most relaxing times I ever had out there. It was my moment of peace in a crazy place.

Our buzz came to an end a few minutes later. Shearer, my former saw gunner and a good friend of mine, was ready to finally take a piss. He walked over to the wall, a wall that happened to be right next to the command center, pulled down his pants, and began to piss all over the wall. Out of nowhere, Captain Shepard appeared from the rooftop of the command center. We must have been loud as hell because we never heard or saw him up there. Fortunately, he didn't know what we were up to. All he saw was Shearer peeing all over the wall. He called down to us asking who was pissing all over his wall. Shearer admitted to it, and as luck would have it, Shepard only yelled at us from a distance and eventually gave Shearer fire watch duty for a few nights. We all hurriedly cleaned up our mess outside, went to bed, and slept soundly through the night.

As for that bottle of vodka, that was a different story. After handing it off to Raymer, he mainly kept it to himself. He did share a couple of sips with some of the other guys, but for the most part, he was the only one to really enjoy that bottle. He paid the price for it though. The person who sent me that vodka had put it in a shampoo bottle; however, the shampoo bottle still contained soap residue. Poor Raymer consumed nearly that whole bottle one night. It would have been fine if it weren't for that residue. The next morning he woke up in extreme pain. We were about to go out on patrol, and he was complaining about pain when he took a piss. A few minutes before we were about to leave, Raymer started peeing blood. He was in extreme pain, so we told him to go to the BAS (medical clinic) on the FOB, and we headed out. Apparently, the soap residue did something to Raymer's stomach that kept him out of commission for the next three days. He made it through it, but he taught us all a lesson: never drink alcohol out of a shampoo bottle.

*****

In every company, there always seems to be certain types of individuals. There's the tough guy who thinks he can take on everyone. There's the moto guy who bleeds red and gold and loves the Marine Corps through and through. There's the smack talker who always talks shit but never backs it up. And then there's the dealer, the guy who's always looking to make a profit out of any situation. Lance Corporal Doug Raymer happened to be our dealer. In fact, he was the whole company's dealer. I'm not sure how he came into it, but Raymer found two areas where he could make money: sunglasses and pills.

Every couple of weeks, Raymer would come around with a piece of paper asking Marines if they wanted to place an order for sunglasses. He had some connection where he could get Oakley sunglasses dirt cheap. Later, I found out that Oakley had a military discount. He would take advantage of the discount and charge a small premium on top of it. By the end of the deployment, the whole company was sporting Oakleys, and some had more than a few pairs.

The other interesting and very odd thing Raymer dealt in was pills. And these weren't any ordinary pills, these were penis-enlargement pills. Close to the beginning of the deployment, we would always see Raymer with a couple of bottles of Magnum Rx. He would religiously take the pills on a daily basis. A few of us were curious about the pills, so he explained the process behind it. You had to take the pills once a day. In order for them to be effective, you also had to do a couple of penis enlargement exercises, mainly yanking on your pecker for about twenty minutes a day. We asked him if it worked, and he said he saw a noticeable difference in a matter of weeks. So with nothing else to keep us occupied, we bought a couple of bottles off of him.

Word began to spread about these pills, and Raymer decided to open up shop. Even Gunny Rossignol got in on it. Raymer was selling Magnum Rx to nearly the whole company. From there on out, Raymer took on a new name, BDR, which was short for Big Dick Raymer. We all figured he was hung like a horse by the end of the deployment because he had taken so many pills. Whether the stuff works or not I have no clue, but I do know that it definitely occupied our time and gave us something to laugh about. There would be nights when I would walk over to the port-a-johns to do my pecker pulling exercises, and I could see lights on in nearly every john. I knew a bunch of other Outlaws were doing the same thing I was about to do. Looking back on it, all I can do is laugh. If the Outlaws are remembered for nothing else, at least we can be recognized as the most well-hung company in the Marine Corps.

# CHAPTER 31
# BOILING POINT

Up until I served in the Marine Corps, I had never experienced the desert heat. I had lived up and down the East Coast when I was a child, but nothing had prepared me for Iraq. When we arrived in February, it was a tolerable eighty degrees. But as the months wore on, the temperature began to increase, hitting highs of 120 degrees. At times, it was so hot that when we did vehicle checkpoints on some of the main service roads, my boots would actually begin to melt into the road. In fact, the insurgents were apparently using this to their advantage when placing IEDs. Word had it that during the heat of the day, they would insert metal underneath the asphalt when it had softened up enough due to the heat. Once it cooled down at night, they would peel it back and place an IED underneath it.

Some days were hotter than others, but there was one day in particular that had to have been the hottest of them all. On June 24, Blue Platoon had gone out for another daily route patrol. They were conducting typical counter IED and mortar patrols that day and were coming to the end of their shift. Our platoon was up next, and we were going to continue where they left off. As luck would have it, and with a little less than an hour before changeover, shit hit the fan. Blue Platoon got word over the company net that an Army convoy was taking fire from a truck stop. They made their way to the location but found nothing there. Suspicious, Rowell decided to double back and have the platoon scout the other side of the highway. Out of nowhere, an RPG was fired at Sergeant Hendrickson's vehicle but, luckily, fell about a hundred meters short and exploded in the sand. Small-arms fire then erupted from the station, but the enemy was hard to see since they were hiding in and around the building. Rowell had the platoon maneuver into a better position to engage the enemy. As they began to counterattack, the enemy, realizing they were outmatched, took off running toward Fallujah.

Realizing what they were trying to do, Hendrickson positioned his vehicle in such a way as to flank them. As he was engaging them, he noticed another insurgent firing at them as he was fleeing between two trucks. As his pintle-mount M247 machine gun was broken, Hendrickson pulled out his M16 and began taking shots at the fleeing insurgent. However, as he was engaging him, the insurgent, who was firing wildly into the air, had a lucky shot that hit Hendrickson. Not realizing he was hit, Hendrickson continued to fire until the insurgent fell to the ground. In the process of reloading, Hendrickson finally realized he was hit. His sleeve was soaked in blood, and he was losing feeling in his arm. Yet, it didn't stop him from continuing on with the mission. For another half hour, they continued to engage the enemy and avoid the mortars that began to pepper their position.

While this was all going down, our platoon began to prep the vehicles for our daily shift. Once we heard the familiar sound of the 25 mm cannon going off in the distance, we knew something was going down. Since the city of Fallujah was only about a kilometer away from our base, it wasn't too hard to hear the battle going on. Once we got word from the command center that Blue Platoon had been engaged, a few of us decided to climb up and sit on the base perimeter wall to see if we could watch the action taking place. A few minutes later, Sergeant Learn came running over and told us to get our shit together. We were going out as soon as possible to relieve Blue Platoon. Blood pumping and adrenaline flowing, we all grabbed our stuff, threw on our gear, and headed over to First Lieutenant Snipes's position. He gave us a quick situation report, informed us as to what Blue Platoon was encountering, and had us mount up so we could join the firefight and give Blue Platoon some relief.

The drive over to Blue Platoon's position was only about ten minutes, but by the time we reached them, they had pushed the insurgents out of the truck stop and back into the sand dunes that lay just behind the buildings. The sand dunes were the only thing left between the truck stop and Fallujah. The insurgents were trying to goad Blue Platoon into the city, where they would have the upper hand. Wisely, Rowell had his platoon set up a position within the truck stop while they continued to engage the enemy from afar.

Snipes pulled his vehicle up alongside Rowell's, and Rowell filled him in on the situation. Once the debrief was over, Rowell called his scouts in and had his platoon pull out of their positions and head back to Camp Fallujah so Hendrickson could be taken care of. Snipes called me over, and he informed Sergeant Jones and me as to the situation and what his plans were. Following in the footsteps of Rowell, Snipes insisted that we not go past the truck stop. He wanted nothing to do with entering the city and getting our vehicles stuck. So he deployed our vehicles in strategic positions where the vehicles had maximum protection but also maximum visibility of the engagement zone. He then had the scouts deploy to provide security for the vehicles as they began to blast away at the enemy positions.

Our vehicle and Sergeant Learn's vehicle set up positions on the far left side of the station while Snipes and Krall were located on the right side. I had my scouts deploy to defensive positions while I surveyed the scene. I saw several weapons that must have been abandoned by the insurgents as they fled. On the other side of the station, Sergeant Jones and his team found some of the dead bodies that had been left behind when Blue Platoon engaged the insurgents within the station.

I continued to do a quick sweep of the area and then set in to a position next to Lance Corporal Raymer. He gave me a quick smirk and then continued to watch the destruction in the distance. The insurgents had pushed even farther back into the sand dunes. There were a couple of buildings that were separated from the city, located within the dunes. The LAVs were concentrating their fire on those buildings. From a distance, I could see insurgents with RPGs and small arms running from building to building trying to take shots at us. It was pointless because they were a good two kilometers away, but every now and then I would hear a stray shot whiz by my head or see an RPG explode well short of our position.

Seeing the insurgents run back and forth while the 25 mm cannons laid into them was amusing. It was like watching a game of duck hunt. The gunners would lay a few rounds in front of one of the enemy positions, and the insurgents would take off to another position, only to double back when the gunners fired at the new position.

After a period of time, Corporal Klinger noticed some insurgents had gotten closer to our position and were hiding behind some sand dunes. While Klinger began to focus his rounds on this new location, Snipes had Sergeant Jones and a couple of scouts find out what was behind the dunes.

Suddenly, the insurgents began to fire off mortars at our position. Fortunately, they couldn't hit the broad side of a barn, but they were still getting close. I could hear some of them fly overhead. It sounded as if someone had thrown a Nerf football with the little whistle in it. All I heard was a whistle, and then somewhere close by, I would hear a thunderous boom. Staff Sergeant Phelps called over to us to get back inside the vehicles. In the meantime, Sergeant Jones and his crew were still downrange when the mortars started landing around them. They hastily made their way back to the vehicles and informed Snipes as to what they had seen. Behind the dunes, they had found several weapons as well as a few injured insurgents. Snipes had the scouts get inside the vehicle but had Doc Barajas stay put.

"Doc," Snipes said, "do you think you can patch up one of the wounded insurgents so we can bring him back for interrogation?"

"Not sure, sir," Doc said in his lazy California accent. "I can give it a shot but I can't guarantee anything. They're pretty fucked up and might not make it back before bleeding out."

"All right. Give it your best shot but don't go out of your way. I don't need you getting hurt helping one of them," Snipes said before turning to Nava.

"Nava, escort Doc to where the wounded insurgents are. While you're out there, grab all the abandoned weapons and blow 'em up with some C4. I don't need their buddies getting their hands on extra rifles."

"No problem, sir," Nava said with a grin creeping across his face. He loved when he got a chance to blow stuff up.

After receiving their instructions, they jumped out of the back of the vehicle and headed over to the weapon cache. Nava had Barajas assist him in digging a hole so they could throw all the weapons in for demolition. Just as they began to break ground, a mortar struck about twenty yards away. Barajas and Nava were knocked off their feet. Nava slowly stood back up and checked to make sure he was still intact. When he realized he was fine, he asked Doc if he was OK. Doc got up and confirmed he was fine, but Nava knew otherwise. Blood was slowly creeping down Barajas's face. A piece of fragmentation must have caught him on the cheek. As it was so small, he must not have noticed it right away. When Nava told him about the small wound, Barajas didn't believe him. It wasn't until he put his hand to his face and wiped away some blood that he knew Nava wasn't kidding. Nava took some of Barajas's medical equipment and gave him a quick field bandage to stop the flow of blood. Once he was patched up, they finished off digging the pit and then blew up the cache. Mortars were still coming in, so they ran back to the vehicle and sat inside.

Back in my vehicle, the heat was getting to be unbearable. As we had battened down all the hatches to the vehicle, the heat inside the vehicle began to increase. It probably didn't help that the vehicle was pure steel and it was 120 degrees that day. It was as if we were getting fried alive. Add to it that our gunners were still engaging the enemy and that the 25 mm cannon emitted its own heat, and you can see why we were so uncomfortable. My scouts and I had cracked open our vests, and we were pouring what little water we had down one another's backs. One of the scouts in our platoon had busted out a digital thermometer, and it read 140 degrees inside the vehicle. I honestly didn't know how long we were going to last being holed up like that. I think I would have rather dodged mortar rounds than get fried alive inside the vehicle.

Fortunately, Snipes had begun to call in air support. He relayed the coordinates of the buildings where the insurgents were hiding to command, and they deployed a few jets with five-hundred-pound bombs. In the distance and above all the other noise, I could hear the jets fly in. Shortly after I heard them fly by, I heard a loud explosion. Sergeant Honigsberg, our gunner, gave a little chuckle. Even though the first bomb had missed, it decimated the area. The jets flew back for another go-around. Snipes relayed adjusted coordinates to the pilots and the second time around, the buildings were completely demolished. Once the air cleared, we waited around to see if more insurgents appeared. When it looked as if there was nothing left to battle, we slowly departed the area and headed back to the base.

Just as in previous firefights, when we got back, Snipes debriefed us and congratulated us for a job well done, and then we made our way back to the hooch. Everyone gave Barajas a little hell for the scratch he got on his face, but it was all in good fun. And, most importantly, we were glad he was alive. The last thing you want to see is one of your own men go down. Our company had enough injuries up until this point, and we didn't need any more.

# CHAPTER 32
# HEAVEN'S DRIVER

IEDs were becoming a more common occurrence as the months wore on. Each day a patrol went out, they either found an IED or one blew up. Fortunately, most of the IEDs that did blow never really did much harm. But when they did find their mark, it never ended well.

IEDs came in all shapes and sizes. Most of the ones we encountered were typically 155 mm artillery shells that were wired up to some sort of device, whether it was a remote detonator or a wired one. For the most part, the IEDs were buried in the ground or hidden within objects, like the one I encountered during the first half of the deployment. However, there were times that the IED was vehicle-borne, like the one that killed Wilfong and Vincent. The vehicle-borne IEDs were less frequent, but they were just as nerve-racking.

A few days after our battle on the east side of Fallujah, Blue Platoon was sent out on another patrol to sweep the main roads for IEDs. About halfway through their patrol, they began patrolling the alternate service routes (ASRs) that were parallel to the road. Soon thereafter, they noticed a suspicious-looking vehicle parked underneath an overpass. The vehicle appeared to be abandoned, and there was no one in the vicinity. When

Second Lieutenant Rowell was informed of the situation, he sent over his scout team to check it out. Sergeant Leuba, the scout leader for the Blue Platoon, cautiously led his team in the direction of the vehicle. About halfway there, they came across a fairly deep creek that they had to cross in order to reach the vehicle. Rowell, deciding that the scouts may be too exposed crossing the creek, decided to call them back so they could regroup and figure out a different way to get to the car. As soon as they turned around and headed back toward Rowell's position, the car exploded, with debris flying everywhere. Rowell and his scouts thanked their lucky stars that they had made that decision. Many fine Marines would have been killed that day if they had continued on. Unfortunately, Blue Platoon wouldn't be so lucky next time.

On July 1, Blue Platoon headed out on another counter-IED sweep. My platoon was acting as the REACT force. We always ended up being the REACT force for Blue Platoon. As part of the REACT force, we had to ensure that our gear and vehicles were ready to go in a moments notice. Once everything was prepped, we sat around in the hooches and either cleaned our weapons or played cards to kill time.

With Sergeant Callendar and Sergeant Hendrickson both wounded and no longer acting as vehicle commanders, Blue Platoon had a few replacements take over on their vehicles. On this particular day, Sergeant Jake Rhinehart and Sergeant Simms took over as vehicle commander and gunner, respectively, for Blue 3. As the platoon headed out for patrol, I gave a quick nod to a couple of the guys and quietly wished for their safety. After having encountered so many IEDs in the last few months, it became a new habit to quietly hope for everyone's safe return back from patrol. It wasn't much, just a few hushed words to myself, but it helped relax my nerves. I headed back to the hooch wondering what I was going to do to kill time.

Blue Platoon was dying to get their patrol done that day. They were scheduled for a little R&R over at Camp Fallujah that afternoon, and everyone was excited to be able to take a dip in the pool they had on the base. The last thing they wanted was for anything to happen that would delay their plans.

Their patrol route was situated about six miles west of Abu Ghraib. They had patrolled up and down the main road for quite a while, so they decided to set up in a screen line position to observe the route and its surroundings, looking for any suspicious activity that may be occurring. After an hour of seeing nothing but sand, they resumed their patrol of the main road.

Right around 11:30 a.m., they began to head back toward Camp Fallujah to wrap up their patrol for the day and get some much-needed R&R. Rowell had the vehicles cross over the intersection and begin heading back. As the platoon began to turn around, Sergeant Rhinehart called over to company headquarters to inform them of their position. In the meantime, Sergeant Simms was bullshitting with Lance Corporal Timothy Creager, the driver, over the internal speaker system about being back home. Creager, a tall, lanky country boy from Tennessee, was telling Simms how he was going to take his city butt out for some bull riding. And that was when it hit.

A bright white flash consumed the interior of the vehicle, and a loud, thunderous boom could be heard from miles around. The vehicle was instantly engulfed in flames. The moment the IED went off, the scouts immediately evacuated the vehicle. Corporal Hall, Corporal Cuba, Lance Corporal Torok, and Doc Ferguson all jumped out onto the road and began to assess the situation. Other than a few burns, scrapes, and bruises, as well as some hearing loss, they all fared relatively well. The vehicle crew was a different story.

The explosion had momentarily knocked Rhinehart and Simms unconscious, and they were both slumped over the sides of the turret. Fire was quickly consuming the vehicle, and they only had a matter of minutes to evacuate the LAV. All around them, rounds were cooking off due to the extreme heat. It sounded as if they were under fire.

Rhinehart, sensing the direness of the situation, began to try to lift himself out of the vehicle so he could make his way to a safer position. As he began to climb, his foot bent back, and he fell back inside the turret. With all of his might, he reached up and lifted himself up out of the turret. Once on the top, knowing his legs would no longer support him, he lay on his side and rolled off the vehicle, landing ten feet below with a thud.

In the meantime, Simms finally came to and realized the situation he was in. He began to try to lift himself out of the turret but felt something tugging him back in. He saw that his comm helmet was still connected to the vehicle, so he ripped off the helmet and made his way out of the turret. Rather than climb down the side, he made his way to the back of the vehicle and decided to jump from that area since it was a bit closer to the ground. He called over to the scouts to catch him, but they were too late in coming. As he was about to jump, a sharp pain shot up through his body, and rather than jumping, he fell right off the back.

Creager, on the other hand, never even made it out of the vehicle. From what I was told later on, no one really knew the exact cause of death. A few of the scouts found what looked like small metal cubes that the bomb maker probably added to the IED to cause maximum damage. Also, after the initial blast, the compressor tank exploded, sending a ball of flame throughout the scout compartment.

Outside, Corporal Justin Hall and Doc Ferguson catered to the burns they received from the compression tank explosion, and then they, along with some of the other scouts, did their best to attend to Rhinehart and Simms. Rhinehart was in very bad shape, with wounds and burns all over his body. By the looks of his face, you could see the pain he was feeling. Simms wasn't as bad but didn't fare too well either. He suffered severe burns as well as a couple of wounds from shrapnel. Surprisingly, though, he seemed to be very calm, most likely due to shock. It wasn't until someone poured cold water on Simms's hands that he let out a yell.

As everyone was tending to Rhinehart and Simms, Rowell pulled his vehicle up alongside the burning vehicle, and the scouts loaded Rhinehart and Simms into the back of the LAV and hurriedly brought them to the Abu Ghraib medical facility. A few days later, they were flown to the States, where they would receive better medical treatment.

Our platoon, as the REACT force, showed up shortly after the explosion to provide relief to Blue Platoon. We had positioned ourselves farther away from Rhinehart's vehicle, but I could still see it burning in the distance, black smoke billowing up into the air. Gunny Rossignol showed up on the scene as well. It's probably a good thing that he did because a contingent of Army personnel came out with a crane and lowboy and didn't seem to understand the care needed for transporting the destroyed LAV. Rossignol explained that an Outlaw was still inside and that they had better ensure that they took great care in putting the vehicle onto the lowboy and transporting it back to Camp Fallujah.

Once the scene was clear, our platoon headed back to Camp Baharia to be debriefed, and Gunny followed the lowboy to Camp Fallujah. He stayed there for quite some time to ensure that mortuary affairs were able to extract Creager's body out carefully. The next day, as he did every time an Outlaw was killed, Gunny would head back to Camp Fallujah to inventory the fallen Outlaw's personal possessions and send them back home.

We finally arrived back at the camp, and I could physically feel the sadness in the air. All the Outlaws were out of the hooches mourning the loss of a brother and the injuries that Simms and Rhinehart sustained. Some were talking to the guys from Blue Platoon trying to find out more information about what had happened.

After a period of time, we were all instructed to gather around the command center so Captain Shepard could talk to us. We made our way over to the area with our heads bowed. We were one more man down; one more brother had been lost. That day was supposed to be a joyous day for Blue Platoon, one in which they let off a little steam and forgot about the hostile environment they were in. Instead, it turned into a day of mourning, a day when one of our own was taken from us.

Shepard came out and gave a short speech. It was nothing memorable, just like most of his speeches. It did nothing to help us through our day of mourning. Thankfully, First Sergeant Sprague followed up with a speech of his own. I may have mentioned it before, but I cannot say it enough: Sprague was one hell of a speaker. He began to speak in a soft tone, slowly recounting how great a Marine Creager was. He spoke about how we, as a company, had lost many fine Marines and how we would overcome such loss. And then he finished off with what I thought was the most memorable part of the speech. He said that God already had two scouts for his LAV, and he was looking for a driver. Those three Marines, our brothers, were now looking down on us and providing us with the security we needed to make it through the rest of our deployment. I may not be a religious man, but it brought a tear to my eye. And from the looks of it, it brought tears to the rest of the company.

I wish I could end it here and say that his prediction was true, that no fellow Outlaws would be harmed. It would have made for a happy ending. But alas, that was never the case. Death was just around the corner, and he had plans for the Outlaws.

# CHAPTER 33
# GRANDPA

When we were back in the States and I was still the company clerk, there were a few Marines who stood out to me when they checked in to the Outlaws. Some I remembered because of their personality. Some I remembered because of their attitude. And then there were some I remembered because I became close to them down the road.

Within the first month of the Outlaws forming, we began to receive a lot of new guys, or what we called boots, who were checking in straight from infantry school or who had only been with the battalion a few months. On one particular day, three PFCs from Alpha Company checked in, and I remember it so well because they all had last names starting with D: Jeremiah Doub, Brett Durbin, and Scott Dougherty. I was only a lance corporal at the time, but they all reported to my desk and stood at parade rest until I told them to chill out. And they all did except the smallest guy in the group, Dougherty.

After I had finished checking Doub and Durbin into the company, I began taking Dougherty's information. Dougherty was this small guy who looked no older than a high school kid. I figured he couldn't be any more than fifteen or so. He just had a very young-looking face. As he stood there at parade rest, I began to take down his personal information to enter into the computer. I would ask him a question, and he would respond, ending each response with a "Lance Corporal." I thought it was crazy that a PFC was addressing me this way since the low-ranking enlisted guys were all on the same boat. So I tried to calm him down, but he wanted none of it. It was as if he was afraid to get in trouble.

I resumed asking questions, and I began to notice another little quirk: he had a stutter. Initially, I thought it was because he was overly nervous. He was sweating, he seemed jittery, and his face was slightly red. As time went on, it got a bit worse. That was when I really started feeling bad. So I ordered him to sit down at the desk next to me so I could finish taking his information. I also instructed him to call me Tanner without the Lance Corporal title. He nodded in the affirmative, sat down, and finally looked more at ease. His stutter also seemed to slowly go away.

From that day on, we struck up a little friendship. I tried to watch over him and get him situated within the company. I started calling him my little son because I felt I was trying to mentor him. Eventually, after Dougherty relaxed a bit and got used to the Outlaw atmosphere, he began to call me Grandpa. For those of you who don't know me, and even for those who do, I have a little problem: I'm follicly-challenged. Gunny Rossignol dubbed me Bobby Bald Spots on my first deployment. It was funny as hell too. So Dougherty, following in Gunny's steps, began to call me Grandpa because of my hair, or lack thereof. I still like to think he looked up to me, even though it might have been the bald spots he kept looking at. In either case, we formed a good friendship.

Another guy who checked in to the Outlaws was Lance Corporal Mark Engel. Mark was a mechanic who had come from another company. When he came to the Outlaws, I knew he'd fit right in. Mark was about my height but with a thicker build. He had a playful and rambunctious personality. He'd call things as he saw them, regardless of rank, which got him in trouble at times. And what I liked most about him was that he was adventurous. Nothing was too crazy an idea to him. He was willing to take risks where others wouldn't. It was truly inspiring.

Mark knew a few of the guys from the company already, guys like Corporal Klinger and Corporal Sprenger. Since I hung around those guys day in and out, I began to get to know Mark as well. He was a blast to hang out with. There were a few times he and I would jump into his Jeep Cherokee, blast some tunes, and head out to the beach. When the four of us went places, I knew it would be a good time because Mark would be the life of the party and would get the rest of us in a party mood. All in all, Mark enjoyed life and inspired others to see the world and life as he saw it.

Throughout our deployment to Iraq, even though some of my buddies were in other platoons and our patrol schedules were different, I made a point to check in on them and hang out for a bit. Sometimes Dougherty and I would goof around talking shit to each other. Other times, Dougherty would come out of the hooch before I was going on patrol and would hand me some Kool-Aid mix that he had gotten from back home to flavor my water. Engel would be in our portion of the hooch almost daily, complaining to us about this or that, telling jokes or just reminiscing about old times. But no matter what, we all checked in on each other and we became closer because of it.

On July 5, 2004, our platoon was scheduled to do our nightly patrol. Our patrol times had shifted to 6:00 p.m. until 2:00 a.m., so I knew I was in for a long, rough night, and I was already looking forward to getting back and sleeping. After Snipes briefed us on the mission for the night, we headed to our vehicles to mount up. I jumped into the back of my LAV, as did the rest of my scouts, and once Staff Sergeant Phelps was settled down in the vehicle commander spot, we were ready to go. All the vehicles went to the staging area right outside of the hooch, and we waited on Snipes to jump into his vehicle.

Dougherty was standing outside the hooch with a few other guys from Second Platoon and noticed we were about to take off. He walked over to my vehicle and, over the rumble of the engine, yelled, "Grandpa, you want some Kool-Aid for your water?" I looked over at him and gave him a smirk and a nod. He quickly walked away into the hooch, and a few seconds later walked out with a huge, zip lock bag of Kool-Aid powder. He poured some of the powder into a bag and then handed the little bag up to me. I thanked him, and he gave a little nod and wished me luck on patrol. That was the last time I saw little Dougherty.

Our patrol was uneventful. We drove up and down the main service road and some of the side roads numerous times and didn't find much of anything. On the nights that there was no action, it became painful to be on patrol. Having been up all day in the heat of the sun and then having to continue to be alert through the wee hours of the night was rough. All I could think about was taking a nice, long snooze on my cot. After what seemed like days, we headed back to Camp Baharia, parked our vehicles, cleaned our gear, and made our way back to our hooch to get some rest.

As our platoon entered Camp Baharia, Second Platoon was heading out for their shift. It was about two in the morning, and it was pitch black outside. Just as we were instructed, Second Platoon's mission was to conduct counter-IED and mortar patrols. Rather than leave the same way we did, they mixed it up a bit and headed over to Camp Fallujah, drove through a portion of it, and then headed out the south gate.

They started their patrol off by heading north toward Abu Ghraib. Instead of taking the main route toward Abu Ghraib, they decided to use the side roads. The one that Second Platoon decided to take had a canal running along its left side, which was why they decided to take it. The insurgents typically liked these types of routes because they presented an opportunity to ambush our patrols. So rather than disappoint, we liked to encourage the fight and patrol these side roads to see if we could fight on our own terms.

This particular night happened to be very dark. The moon was barely visible, and there were few stars in the sky. It was quiet and peaceful and almost made you forget that we were in the middle of a war zone. As was typical with night patrols, no lights were allowed when traveling these routes. Everyone was equipped with night vision goggles (NVGs), and the vehicles had both night vision and thermal imaging. As they were traveling along the feeder route, the road made a slight right to the east and crossed over the canal. The lead vehicle, White 2, crossed over and began to move east. Shortly thereafter, Lieutenant Kevin Knox Nunnally's vehicle, White 1, and

Staff Sergeant Michael Woods's vehicle, White 3, crossed over and followed White 2.

BA-BOOM!

The dark night turned to day as a tremendous explosion shook the earth, sending up a huge cloud of fire and smoke. It was so loud and so bright that some of the guys back at Baharia heard and saw it.

At first, no one was sure what had happened. Nunnally thought they had come under attack and began to call back to the command center to inform them of the ambush. He sent White 2 into a blocking position on the east side of the blast and moved his vehicle onto the west side, creating a defensive perimeter around the blast site. It wasn't too much longer before Nunnally and the rest of Second Platoon realized what happened. White 4, Sergeant Nicholas Santiago's vehicle, never made it over the canal crossing.

Once it was reported back to the command center what had happened, Lance Corporal Duarte came running into our hooch and told us Second Platoon had been hit. He had a shocked look on his face and was trying to get us up and ready to head back out. I was just getting ready to lie down on my cot and was in no mood for one of his pranks. I wasn't alone either. Duarte was known as a prankster, so everything he said you had to second guess because you never knew if he was playing a trick. Everyone else began to tell him to pipe down and save his pranks for another time. However, when we began to study the look on his face, we could tell he was serious. I'm not sure why Third Platoon wasn't on QRF that night, but it didn't matter. Everyone in our platoon jumped up and began gearing back up to get out there and respond.

Within fifteen minutes, we had all gotten dressed, started our vehicles, and were ready to go. It was only another twenty minutes before we made it to the site of the blast. As we approached the scene, we could sense the devastation in the air. There was a peculiar smell that permeated the air, and bullets were cooking off left and right. My vehicle pulled up within a hundred yards of the blast site. My scouts and I dismounted and began to take up a defensive spot around the scene.

When I finally got everyone settled down, I glanced over at the vehicle and was awestruck by the destruction that had occurred. The vehicle had flipped upside down from the blast, and its scout doors were wide open. The interior was a charred mess. The area around the vehicle was littered with rounds that were cooking off, and anything that was in the vicinity was burned to a crisp. To the left side of the vehicle, I saw a charred body in the upright position leaning against it. I wasn't quite sure who it was, but it didn't matter. All I knew was that I had lost a lot of good friends that day.

After Nunnally had briefed Lieutenant Snipes, Snipes got the rest of the platoon into a defensive perimeter around the scene so we could take over for Second Platoon as they made their way back to Baharia. Sergeant Jones and I met up at the scene of the blast along with Snipes, and I was given a brief summary of what had happened. I probably would have found out more had it not been for the ammo box of rounds about ten feet from us cooking off. That was when Snipes told us to clear the area and find some cover.

We were told that a mortuary team and a lowboy truck were on the way to the scene, so we had to stay put. I got back into position behind a mound with Lance

Corporal Shearer by my side. I just sat there looking out into the distance, not really seeing anything. It was as if nothing was registering anymore; all I could think about was the body on the side of the vehicle and my friends who had been inside of it. I thought of Engel and the picture that he, Sprenger, and I were supposed to take of a Hooters flag on the top of the command center. I thought of Dougherty and how he had just given me flavored powder only a few hours ago. I thought of Corporal Jeffrey Lawrence, who was telling everyone that his wife was due to give birth any day now. I thought of PFC Rodricka Youmans, who had a little boy at home and was planning to get married to his fiancé when we got back. And I thought of Lance Corporal Justin Hunt, a big, jolly guy who always had a smile on no matter what was thrown his way. The images of these five guys kept running through my head over and over again, like a broken record.

The sun began to creep up over the horizon, which was when I finally began to come back to reality. Captain Shepard had arrived at the scene and was walking around inspecting the area and talking to each of us. He came upon Shearer's and my position and asked us how we were doing. I could see the pain in his face, and I'm sure he could see mine. Shearer and I both gave a quick nod, and Shepard continued on his way.

Once the mortuary team showed up, I just sat and watched as they began to load bodies into black bags and put them on the truck. That blank stare came back, and I began to get tunnel vision. Everything around me became blurred, and I just began to focus on each of the bags as they were loaded onto the truck. Once they were all loaded, the vehicle itself was lifted and placed on the lowboy to be taken back to Camp Fallujah. When the scene was cleared, we loaded into our vehicles and headed back to Baharia.

When we got back, it felt as if we were arriving at a funeral. Everyone seemed to be totally taken aback by the whole situation. We had just suffered a great loss five days ago, and this was totally unexpected. A few of the guys from Second Platoon were huddled in a circle praying. Some other guys had tears running down their face.

After we parked our vehicles and put our gear away, I headed over to Sergeant Travis Madden to find out how this all had happened. He began to lay out the details, which I had already found out earlier, but then he told me where it had occurred. That was when I realized our platoon had passed over the same spot earlier that evening. Apparently, everyone in Second Platoon had barely missed it as well, but White 4 must have had a tire run over the spot, and that was what set it off. Also, the IED was no ordinary IED. It was an anti-tank mine that was modified with some sort of liquid that acted like napalm. When White 4 ran over it, the sheer impact of the explosion shot Sergeant Santiago, Corporal Gabriel Wakanabo, and Lance Corporal Engel out of the vehicle like bottle rockets. Santiago and Wakanabo landed in the canal and suffered significant shrapnel injuries, mainly to their legs as well as some burns.

Engel was badly burned in the explosion and was found on the north side of the road. Nunnally had called in a medivac for Engel before we arrived. When it arrived, Doc Weldon, Second Platoon's corpsman, assisted in bringing him to the helicopter. Apparently, Engel never lost his great sense of humor because as Doc was helping to load him onto the helicopter, Engel looked at Weldon, and rather than complain about the pain or ask if he was going to make it, he asked him if his penis was still there. Weldon chuckled and told him it was, to which Engel let out a sigh of relief. We later found out that Engel suffered third-degree burns to over 60 percent of his body and also scorched the inside of his lungs. He was taken to Germany a couple of days later to receive additional treatment where he would later pass away with family surrounding him. Lawrence, Hunt, Youmans, and Dougherty were most likely killed by the initial blast, as they were confined to the scout compartment of the vehicle and had little chance of escaping.

First Sergeant Sprague came out later that day and had us all gather around the command center. Once again, as he always did, he gave another inspiring speech. As each word left his mouth, I could tell it was becoming harder for him to say the next word without breaking down. Nearly the whole company was sobbing or shedding tears. I looked over and saw the biggest guy of us all, Corporal Keith Bridges, physically shaking from the sadness of our loss. The impact of the loss of our brothers that day, as well in days past, was beginning to take its toll on us.

We all headed back to our hooches to mourn some more. Sprenger and I headed back to our cots, and we sat across from each other looking at each other waiting for someone to say something. Sprenger finally broke down and began to sob, and then I did alongside him. A few others joined in as well. We all had lost good friends that day. Some were closer to the fallen than others, but we were all Outlaws, and the losses hurt all the same.

It wasn't too long before someone updated the Outlaw memorial. At the base of the memorial now stood eight plaques for each of the Outlaws we had lost. Tributes would appear on the memorial, and guys could be seen kneeling in front of it paying their respect.

We had been through so much together as a company up to that point, and we would endure a lot more in the final months. The loss of a fellow Marine affected us all, and those five men, along with the three others who passed before, will never be forgotten, for they were our brothers.

# CHAPTER 34
# COMPLACENCY

I was never sure what affected me more: the sight of seeing good friends killed or dealing with the aftermath, of not having those familiar, friendly faces around to talk to and goof around with. What I didn't know up until that day was that Gunny Rossignol dealt with this every time an Outlaw passed away.

From our perspective as the boots on the ground, we saw the aftermath of the incident, our fallen brothers killed in action. When we got back to base, we each dealt with the loss in our own separate way. For those who were close to the dead, the losses were tough to deal with. However, due to the situation we were in, none of us had much time to mourn; we had a mission, and we couldn't let the situation overcome us. The time to mourn for our brothers would come when we got back to the States.

What I found out the day after White 4 was hit was that Gunny Rossignol had to continue to relive the loss of one of his sons for a few more hours. Every time an Outlaw was killed, Gunny was there to ensure the body was transported back to Camp Fallujah safely. He would then have the fallen Marine's belongings boxed up. Once the items were boxed up, he would personally escort them over to the supply center on Camp Fallujah to be inventoried and sent back home.

The day after White 4 was hit and a lot of good friends were taken from us, Gunny came to me and asked if I would help him inventory the belongings of those who were killed. He informed me that he didn't want to ask any of the Marines from White Platoon because it may have been too hard to deal with. After he asked the question, I knew how difficult a task it would be to take on the challenge. It was not as if it were hard, laborious work. Instead, it was emotionally exhausting. Looking into Gunny's eyes, I could see how hard this was for him and how much he needed some help with it, if nothing more than to have company. So I agreed.

I grabbed my flak, helmet, and rifle and met up with Gunny in the Humvee. In minutes, we departed the gates of Baharia and made our way over to Camp Fallujah with all the boxes of personal items in tow. Camp Fallujah was only a quick five-minute drive from Baharia, but this drive seemed to take an eternity. Aside from some small banter, we stayed silent the whole way over.

When we arrived at the supply center on Camp Fallujah, we quickly dismounted our Humvee and began to make our way over to the building where we would unload the boxes. A lance corporal from the supply unit was sitting outside the building on top of an MRE box with no blouse on. Gunny and I walked up to him, and Gunny asked a few questions in regard to who the point of contact was and what we needed to do to get started. The lance corporal gave some half-assed answers and barely gave Gunny the proper respect he deserved, hardly coming to his feet when Gunny approached him.

Just as we were about to go back to the Humvee to start unloading, I looked to the side and saw a flak jacket on a cross in front of a makeshift supply area. Written on to the cross was a common message that was repeated over and over again to all of us: Complacency Kills. We heard this so often because our superiors didn't want us to become complacent and get killed on patrols because we weren't being vigilant. So initially, the message barely even registered in my mind. It wasn't until I took a second glance at the flak jacket and noticed the name tag sewn into the flak: Engel. My jaw dropped to the floor. Here was a guy who gave it his all day in and day out, and this son of a bitch had the audacity to hang a flak jacket of a Marine, not to mention one of my Outlaw brothers and good friend, on a cross and say his death was due to complacency.

I was infuriated. I called over to Gunny to take a look at it, and his face went red. Gunny marched his way over to the lance corporal and began to tear in to him. Gunny made him come to attention, and as he continued to tear into him, calling him every name under the sun, you could see the Marine realize he had messed with the wrong guy.

The lance corporal, when he was given permission to speak, explained that he hadn't realized the significance of the vest nor realized how it had come into his possession. Gunny tore into him some more, saying that no Marine deserved the disrespect that was shown, let alone a fellow Outlaw. After a few more minutes of ass-chewing, Gunny had the Marine take down the flak jacket and bring it inside.

Still seeing red, we made our way back to the Humvee and began to unload the boxes into a storage area. Once we had all the boxes accounted for, we began to open up each one so we could inventory them. As I opened each box, a sea of memories washed over me. Most of the items were articles of personal clothing that we had to account for. The most difficult part was accounting for the pictures of the fallen Marines or photos of loved ones that they kept to remind them of home while deployed. Letters from wives or family members were also hard to look at. As we inventoried each item, Gunny or I would call over to each other to recall a memory of the fallen. It really hurt to think that these items were the last bits of our brothers that we would come in contact with. And it hurt even more to think that these boxes would be shipped back to the family members, and it would be all they had left of their sons, brothers, or fathers.

That was when I realized that Gunny had to do this each and every time an Outlaw was killed. I then understood why this was probably the hardest thing Gunny had to do during our deployment. He saw and treated each of us like his son. He became emotionally attached to each one of us and knew a lot about us without us ever knowing. I could tell him something about myself, and then several months later, he would recall it. It was that kindness and that care that allowed all of us to grow close to Gunny as well as him grow close to us. So when one of our guys was wounded or killed, it really took an emotional toll on Gunny. Sitting there, packing boxes and watching Gunny, I could tell he was on the verge of tears.

When we inventoried and packed the last of the boxes, Gunny had to sign some papers that would be sent home with the boxes. Gunny would later tell me that the hardest thing for him to do was to sign those papers because the fallen's loved ones would see his name included with the boxes that were sent to them. Maybe that's why it hurt so badly.

For me, packing those boxes was like finally admitting that my friends had passed. It had a sense of finality, as if I were saying good-bye to them. If it weren't for Gunny holding it together, I might have broken down in tears. Instead I gathered up my belongings, and Gunny and I made our way back to the Humvee. We passed by the cross on our way back, but this time around, there was no flak jacket on the cross. Later that day, Sergeant Flaherty and his crew would come back to the building and see it again. However, this time around would take it by force, bringing back Engel's flak jacket as if they were bringing their brother back to his final resting ground.

Those boxes continued to bother me far into the future. It hurt knowing that it was the last time I would see my friends. It bothered me even more knowing that the box was the last thing family members would receive of their loved one. Now I knew the pain that Gunny felt every day. Now I knew why our deployment had aged him beyond his years.

# CHAPTER 35
# ROAD TRIP

Shortly after the devastating loss of so many of our fellow Outlaws, our company was taken off the road for a brief period of time to recoup. The death count had finally begun to wear on our psyche, and I was beginning to see cracks in some individuals. So the brief rest was a good thing. In fact, during that week of rest, the platoons were each given a two-day stay over at Camp Fallujah.

To some this wasn't much, but to those of us who had been doing the daily grind day in and day out, those two days seemed like a stay at Disney World. Camp Fallujah was no resort, but it did have quite a few amenities that we had very little exposure to over in Camp Baharia. For one thing, we were allowed to shack up in air-conditioned buildings, something that was unheard of over at Baharia. On top of that, we were able to do whatever we wanted over in the camp, so long as we ensured we were back in time for fire watch. Most of us hit up the game room or the PX to stock up on more snacks and goodies. Everyone made sure to make a stop at the chow hall. The chow hall at Camp Fallujah was like a four-star restaurant compared to the chow tent we had at Baharia. It was open nearly all day long, they served hot, fresh meals, and we could drink all the soda we wanted. And last but not least, there was the pool, a hidden oasis in the middle of the desert that was a true treat. It was hard enough to get a shower, let alone swim in a pool.

Those two days our platoon spent there were some of the most relaxing and carefree times I had in Iraq. Gone were the everyday worries of dying. All I could think about was how full my stomach was and how nice it was there. But that all soon came to an end. After about a week off the patrols, our company was tasked with a new mission.

Captain Shepard gathered us around one day and informed us we were being tasked with assisting the Army down in Iskandariyah, a town about fifty miles south of Baghdad. A couple days prior, the Army base in Iskandariyah had been hit by mortars. Apparently, this attack set a good portion of the hooches in the compound on fire. As if that weren't bad enough, most of those hooches contained equipment and other gear that was destroyed by the fire. So our presence was requested to relieve them of their duties while they regrouped and got themselves back in working order. Our week of rest and relaxation had come to an end. It was time to get back to work.

After receiving word that we would be going, everyone dispersed to get ready for the trip. From what we understood, we would be there anywhere from two weeks to a month. So pretty much everything we had in our hooch needed to come with us. I went back to my hooch and gathered up all the essentials: clothing, cammies, gear, snacks, and cigs. I did my best at packing it all into my rucksack and the carry-on bag that we were allowed to bring with us. Once I was done packing, I hauled everything over to my vehicle and rigged it up to the outside of it. After I was done, I went around to help out some of the other guys. I figured the faster we got packed up, the faster we could get down there. I absolutely hated sitting around. But, as usual, once we were all packed up and ready to go, we had to sit around and wait until we received permission to leave.

When the word finally came that we needed to head out, it was pitch black except for a little bit of illumination from some of the stars in the nighttime sky. Everyone went to his respective vehicle, did final vehicle and gear inspections, and then mounted up. The vehicles fired up their engines, and you could hear a loud rumble permeate the air. The vehicle commanders got the LAVs into a tactical column near the base entrance, and we waited for the final word from Captain Shepard to move out.

In the meantime, we were instructed that the drive down to Iskandariyah was to be in blackout conditions, which meant that no visible light was permitted from the vehicles. So all the vehicles flipped on their infrared lights, and when I donned my night vision goggles, I could see a column of lights behind me. Captain Shepard emerged from the COC and lowered himself into his turret. He jumped on the company communications frequency and gave the word to move out. One by one, each vehicle made its way out of the base and began the trek down to Iskandariyah.

Our journey down to the town was uneventful. For miles on each side of the road, all I could see was the vast, barren desert intermingled with a couple of shacks here and there. A few cars would come zooming up to the column, see us, have multiple guns aimed at them, and then zoom past in a hurry. But aside from that, it was a very boring ride.

Fifty miles doesn't seem like much to the casual driver, but when you're traveling that far in a convoy of LAVs, it can take forever. To begin with, the speed at which our convoy was traveling varied between twenty to forty miles an hour. This was because we had to ensure our speed was not constant, or anyone watching us could time us and hit the convoy with a well-placed IED. In addition to the variation in speed, we also had to stop every once in a while to do maintenance checks on the vehicles to ensure they were operating smoothly. At these stops, all the scouts would get out and set up a defensive perimeter, the drivers would do a quick maintenance check, and the rest of the Marines would stretch their legs, take a piss on the side of the road, or grab a quick bite to eat. So the trip took several hours—several long, boring hours. If it weren't for the fact that I was able to switch out with some of the other scouts standing up in the scout hatch, my knees would have been shot and so would theirs.

After a few hours of driving, I knew we were getting closer because the terrain was changing. There seemed to be a bit more vegetation in the area, and more people were out on the streets. And that was when I saw them—three huge smoke towers sticking up two or three hundred feet in the air, belching out nasty, black smoke. They were monstrous. I thought to myself how it must suck to live near that thing. Not only did they give insurgents a target to drop mortars on, but the smoke belching out of their stacks didn't look too healthy. Fortunately, I thought, we wouldn't be anywhere near there.

As we continued to drive, I noticed a few Iraqi soldiers in the street guarding various intersections. It was one of the very few times I actually saw some of these guys doing something other than training. The towers continued to grow as we approached them, but it wasn't until we were passing through another checkpoint that it dawned on me that those towers were our final destination. Just our friggin' luck.

Thirty minutes or so passed by, and we finally pulled up to our new home, a giant oil power plant that provided over sixty percent of Iraq's electricity needs. All around, soldiers were moseying about, looking carefree as they walked to and fro. Some of them weren't even walking around with their flak and weapon. What the hell was going on around here? Did they not realize this was a war zone? The situation was starting to piss me off, and it would only get worse.

We rolled up to a giant hangar bay and pulled to a halt. This was where we were staying for the next few weeks. Inside was filled with hundreds of cots, our new beds, and that was about it. At least it was somewhat cool in there. The last thing we wanted was to be stuck in a musty, humid hangar with no ventilation.

We began to unload our gear and settle into our new home. I threw what I had brought with me underneath my cot, grabbed my flak and rifle, and stepped outside the hangar to get a good look at our new surroundings. About a quarter of a mile to the right of us was the internet center. Slightly behind us was a massive chow hall. And smack dab in the middle of the whole compound were the three giant smoke stacks that just so happened to be only a few hundred feet from our hangar.

No wonder why the Army had lost a bunch of gear. They had picked a giant friggin' target as a base.

As if things couldn't get any worse, I began to notice that the air had a weird odor to it. After further investigation, I figured out that the odor was coming from the power plant itself. Iraq does not have the same stringent environmental rules that we do, so I'm pretty sure that however they were burning the oil to generate electricity was probably not good for anyone living around the plant. After a couple of weeks into our stay there, my lungs felt as if they were coated with something, and it wasn't until several months after we were back stateside that I could breathe without hacking up a lung.

Iskandariyah, in my eyes, sucked, and all I wanted was for the Army to get its act together and get up and running so we could get back to our life in Baharia. By the end of the day, Fallujah looked like paradise.

# CHAPTER 36
# BLACK CLOUD

It was as if our stay in Iskandariyah was destined to be miserable from the get-go. The Outlaws had begun to settle down in our little hellhole. We were debriefed by the Army unit that we were replacing on what the current situation was and how they had been conducting operations on a daily basis. To sum it up, they were doing limited excursions that went no farther than about one or two miles from the base. This infuriated the whole company. No wonder they got mortared on a daily basis. They were doing it to themselves by not directly engaging the enemy. But it was not our job to judge, it was only our job to complete the mission at hand. So we quickly began making our presence known in the local community by conducting daily patrols far outside the normal boundaries of operation.

A few days into our stay, the first set of bad news hit. I was sitting on my cot inside the hangar chatting with Sprenger and Klinger. One of the junior Marines in our company called over to tell us that Lieutenant Snipes wanted to pass word to the platoon. No one was exactly sure what it was all about. There was hope that it had something to do with going back to Baharia. The Marines from First Platoon slowly rose and made their way to

Lieutenant Snipes's position outside the hangar. We all gathered in a semi-circle around him. Sprenger, Klinger, and I were standing off to one side of the circle, and we could tell that whatever the news was, it wasn't good. Something about the look on Lieutenant Snipes's face gave me a sick feeling. When Snipes was sure that the whole platoon had arrived, he began to speak in a low, sorrowful voice.

"We received word that Lance Corporal Engel passed away at a hospital in Germany." That's all I remember hearing for what seemed like an eternity. In the back of my head, I had been hoping beyond hope that Mark would be able to survive his injuries and make it through this alive. I kept telling myself over and over from the day he was injured that he would be all right. Even when the logical part of me would try to bring me back down to reality, the optimistic side would hold on to that small shimmer of hope. So the minute Lieutenant Snipes uttered those words, reality came crashing down to give me a gut check. It seemed as if I were paralyzed in time. So many good memories of Mark flashed before my eyes, and I could hardly move as I saw them slowly fade away.

Lieutenant Snipes's voice came flooding back in after a short while. He was explaining some of the details of Mark's death. He informed us of the severity of the wounds that Mark had sustained and how he seemed to be making progress but eventually succumbed to the wounds. The one good bit of news, if you could even call it that, was that his parents were able to fly out to be by his side in Germany before he passed. That was the only piece of decent news that didn't make the whole ordeal absolutely terrible.

After Lieutenant Snipes finished talking to us, everyone dispersed, looking for some place to go to digest the news. Klinger, Sprenger, and I headed back to our cots. A few tears were slowly making their way down our faces as we dealt with what we had learned. I couldn't say much. All I could think about were good memories of Mark and how bad I felt for his family to have to watch their son pass away before their eyes. That is a pain I would never wish upon anyone, and to know it happened to the family of a good friend hurt deeply. Sprenger and Klinger were taking the news bad as well. Having been around him longer than I, they had even more good memories of Mark, and knowing that they would never be able to continue to share them with him had visibly shaken them.

I could see that the rest of the company had just received the update, too. Several prayer circles had formed throughout the hangar, a few guys had tears rolling down their faces, and a few others just seemed distant. The news really hurt us all.

About a half hour later, some of the Marines began to leave the hangar to get it off their minds. A few of us went to the chow hall to get some grub before we headed over to the internet center. The whole time, I could see everyone had gone internal, with very little chatter over our meal. The rest of the day went on in roughly the same manner. I went to sleep that night reliving so many moments with Mark, and I'm sure many of the other guys did the same. In fact, years later, Mark still visits in my dreams, and I can still hear his laughter and see his good-natured grin.

# CHAPTER 37
# IED DEPOT

As we settled into our new stomping grounds in Iskandariyah, our company began to set up patrols in and around the city and farther out into the outskirts where we believed the insurgents had been setting up firing positions to mortar the base. The schedule of patrols was set up so that there was one platoon that stayed on the outskirts for about four to five days, and the remaining platoons were either on maintenance and rest, or they were doing limited excursions into and around Iskandariyah for about eight to ten hours a day. My platoon happened to get a lucky draw and got to stick around the base for a few days, and then we began to rotate patrols with the other platoon that remained behind within the city limits.

The first patrol we went on within the city limits definitely had a much different feel from the patrols we were conducting in Fallujah. One noticeable thing was that since the base was located pretty much within the city, our patrols began within the city and made their way to the city limits and sometimes a bit farther. The patrols in Fallujah were typically conducted outside of the city, with the occasional few going inside to provide support to another battalion.

I also noticed that there was much more of an Iraqi army presence here than most of the other places we had conducted operations. However, it wasn't as if their presence put my nerves at ease. Most of them were very poorly equipped, with some form of makeshift body armor and a lopsided helmet. The only two things that indicated some sort of order and uniformity were the standard-issue AK-47 rifles and the camouflage that each of them wore. Aside from that, they resembled more of a militia than an actual army. Fortunately, most of them were only acting as security for vehicle checkpoints, and a good number of them were accompanied by US armed forces counterparts.

We hadn't gone more than about three or four miles from the base when we finally reached the outskirts of the city. We turned off the main highway and began patrolling down a dirt road, which was most likely another main road, but definitely not something we were accustomed to back in the States. We were only about three of four hundred yards down this road when we came upon one of the craziest things I had ever seen during my whole time out in Iraq. Smack dab on the side of the road were hundreds upon hundreds of unexploded ordinance (UXO), from mortars to 155 artillery shells, stacked in a pile, with many more littering the ground for at least one hundred feet from the pile. I was absolutely dumbfounded. This was like the Home Depot of IEDs. No wonder the Army was getting shelled on a daily basis! If they had even bothered to patrol more than a mile outside of their base, they could have found this out for themselves.

After my frustration quickly subsided, I realized Lieutenant Snipes was calling over to our vehicle to have my team and I, along with Sergeant Jones's team, escort our engineer, Sergeant Alfonso Nava, out to the IED stash to figure out what to do with it. I grabbed my scouts, and we carefully made our way over to the UXOs, ensuring not to step on anything that could blow us sky high. As we came closer to the area, it seemed as if the sand was littered with even more UXOs than I had initially realized. However, our biggest concern wasn't the smaller mortars; it was the much larger artillery shells, which were always being used for IEDs.

Nava surveyed the scene and decided it would be best if we handled it ourselves rather than call back to have EOD blow it all up. He had us all begin collecting the artillery shells in the area and stack them up in a pyramid. I think I counted somewhere around thirty or forty by the time we finally finished stacking them. Nava inspected the pile to make sure it was sturdy and wouldn't easily fall over. He then began to prep the area by laying out a long string of C4 explosives all along the top of the pile. He laid out approximately eight or nine bricks of C4 in a row lengthwise across the top and readied them all with detonation (det) cord and primers. Once he was certain the pile was ready to go, he had us all go back to our vehicles, and he hastily made his way back to his with the det cord trailing behind him.

Lieutenant Snipes called over the radio for everyone to move outside of the blast radius. The roar of the LAV engines came to life, and all the vehicles moved just outside the blast radius but remained close enough for us to respond to any potential event that could occur before the blast. Snipes began a countdown over the radio, and a few seconds before the detonation, everyone was ordered to sit down inside the vehicles so we wouldn't be hit by any stray object.

Snipes counted down the final seconds, "Three…two…one…"

BOOOOOOOOOOMMMMMMM!

Even inside the LAV, I could feel the blast of the explosion. It violently shook the vehicle for a second or two before there was calm again. I stood up and peered out of the top of my scout hatch and saw a grayish-black mushroom cloud billowing into the sky. The pile of potential IEDs was obliterated, and in its place was a big black mark on the ground where the shells had been.

Snipes reported back to our command center that the shells were destroyed. He also informed them that there were still hundreds of small UXOs (unexploded ordinance) that needed to be dealt with. A few days later, the Army would send out some EOD personnel to clean up the area.

We continued on with our patrol that day, and I felt a bit better knowing that we had destroyed a good number of potential IEDs that could have killed my brothers. However, in the back of my mind I knew that even though we wiped out a large number of artillery shells that day, there were always more lurking out there. In the ensuing days, we would continue to get hit by multiple IEDs on our patrols. It just reminded us that the threat was always out there, and we had to remain vigilant and aware at all times.

# CHAPTER 38
# HOUSE RAID

We had been in Iskandariyah for a little over two weeks, and it was finally our turn to stay out in the field for an extended amount of time, which was supposed to be about four or five days. I had grown accustomed to doing our daily patrols and then getting some R&R back at the base, eating a decent meal, and going to the PX on a daily basis, so going out into the field didn't appeal to me too much at the time. A day before we were going to move out, everyone began to stock up on snacks and cigs to hold us over for the four days we were told we were going to be out there. I made sure to send out a few e-mails to family, stocked up on some good snacks so I could avoid eating MREs, and bought about four or five packs of cigarettes. We were told not to pack everything since we would be back in a few days, so I left some of my belongings in the hangar so I wouldn't have to carry around so much weight and so I could carry more snacks. Smart thinking on my part, or so I thought.

The morning of our departure into the far outskirts of the city was upon us, and it began with the arrival of White Platoon coming back from their stint out there. They looked worn out, filthy, and in much need of some rest. Lieutenant Nunnally and Lieutenant Snipes spoke briefly, and then Snipes came back to our section of the hangar to give us a briefing on how we were going to proceed out to our area of operation. Once he finished speaking, we gathered up our belongings, mounted or stored them in the vehicle, and then got in the vehicles, ready to begin our journey to our outpost.

Shortly after we got into our vehicles, Lieutenant Snipes's voice came over the radio to ensure everyone was good to go. Once all the vehicle commanders rogered up, he gave the signal to move out. The engines of all the vehicles came to life almost simultaneously, and we began to move forward.

The journey was uneventful and seemed as if it only took about a half hour. Our destination was nothing special, really, just a small patch of grass in the middle of a palm-grove-type area, with vegetation and small farming canals surrounding us. About a mile away was a small farming village, and in the near distance, you could easily see the smokestacks from the power plant towering into the sky.

Once we assessed the area to ensure it was safe, the vehicles set up in a defensive 360 perimeter, and everyone dismounted. I, along with Staff Sergeant Phelps and a few other Marines, headed over to Lieutenant Snipes's position to get an idea of what we were going to do next. He gave us a quick rundown of what our mission would be over the next few days. It was fairly simple. We would be conducting several daily foot patrols in and around our area in order to deter any insurgents from mounting mortar attacks or planting IEDs. Half of the scouts would remain at our outpost, and the others would go out on patrol.

Once Lieutenant Snipes finished with his orders, we dispersed and went back to our vehicles. Everyone began to settle down into our new spot. Some guys broke out MREs, others began maintaining their rifles or vehicles, and the rest of us just goofed around until the patrols began.

Sergeant Jones took his scout section out first. I watched as they formed up and began heading out toward the canals. I gave several scouts a nod and wished them luck and turned back to do whatever nonsense I was doing to keep myself busy. A few minutes later, I peered back in the direction they had gone and watched as the last scout in the patrol walked through tall reeds that were on the banks of the nearest canal.

A few hours later, Sergeant Jones and his group came back and debriefed Lieutenant Snipes. They had seen nothing out of the ordinary, so there wasn't really much to discuss. A few Marines from Jones's section came over to give us an idea of what they had seen, and it really didn't seem like much—just a bunch of canals that were waist deep and a lot of nothingness in the surrounding area.

About an hour after Jones's section came back, Lieutenant Snipes had me prepare my section for patrol. I gathered up all my scouts, did a quick glance over their gear, and made sure everyone was ready to move out. We briefly met with Lieutenant Snipes to get an idea of what he wanted us to do and then formed up into a tactical column. I gave my point man, Lance Corporal Zabala, a rundown of what the plan was for the patrol and headed back toward the middle of the column. Staff Sergeant Phelps decided he wanted to tag along with us on the patrol, so he grabbed his gear and an extra M-16 and made his way toward my location. I briefly ran him through the plan, he acknowledged, and I gave Zabala the signal to move out.

The patrol was absolutely boring. The only thing that really stood out was the many canals we had to wade through. For me, a six-foot guy, it was fairly easy because at the highest point, the water only made it up to mid-stomach. For some of the shorter guys, the water was pretty close to chin level. I had some of the other Marines help the shorter guys out by supporting them as they made their way to the other side. But aside from the canals, our patrol was uneventful.

These patrols and periods of boredom went on for the next few days. We'd mix the patrols up daily just to keep the Marines alert and on their toes. Sometimes we'd conduct them right at dawn, or we'd send out some midnight patrols. But during the time we were out there, nothing ever happened, which kind of bummed us all out.

Toward the end of our stay at our outpost, we were all getting antsy to get back to the base. Cigarettes and snacks were running low, guys wanted to contact friends and family back home, and tempers were beginning to run a bit high. So everyone was really looking forward to our last day out there. Except that it wasn't. Our last day out in the field, word was passed down that the whole company would be coming out to our location. This was the last thing anyone wanted to hear. All we wanted to do was go back and replenish our supplies, but we were overruled.

Sometime that afternoon, the rest of the Outlaws, to include Headquarters and Weapons Platoons, met up with us out in the field. At that point, everyone who was low on snacks and cigarettes in our platoon began begging to grab some from the other guys who had just come out. Fortunately, most of them were generous and hooked us up.

No one was quite sure why the whole company was now out there. It didn't appear there was any threat to deal with. However, our job was not to question, it was to follow orders. The one thing that did change was that we moved our outpost slightly closer to the farming village. I was guessing that was the point of the whole company coming out, but again, I wasn't told the exact reason why.

Patrols commenced again, but our platoon was given a bit of a break since we had been doing them the last few days. The patrols mainly covered the areas that we had already been patrolling before, but there were some that began skirting the small village.

After a few days of the whole company being out there, it became apparent that our mission was to gather intel on the small village. One afternoon, Lieutenant Snipes brought the platoon together to give us a new set of orders. We were to conduct a patrol into the town itself. None of the vehicles would be accompanying us, but they would be within a half-mile in case anything happened. He gave us a layout village and began delegating responsibility to the various scout teams. As I was the only scout who spoke limited Arabic, I was assigned to accompany the intel officer who was attached to our company for the patrol, and provide security as well as some form of interpretation. Fortunately for me, we were also given a local interpreter who could assist in talking with the villagers.

In addition to my scout section, a couple of other scout teams from White and Blue Platoon were going to be accompanying us. They were all briefed the same information I was given. Essentially, our mission was to gather intel on the village and determine if there were any insurgents in or around the area. It seemed like an easy enough mission at a glance. My only concern was that there was only one main road going into the village, and it was surrounded by buildings on both sides. It also didn't help that the locals had been giving us evil stares the last few days either.

Once everyone was set to go, the various scout teams formed up into a tactical column, and we began to make our way to the village. We moved from our outpost, which was about half a mile away from the village, over rocky, lopsided terrain, and finally began approaching the village. Once the townspeople saw us, some of them began hurrying out of sight. This really unnerved me. I felt we were about to be ambushed.

A few minutes later, we stepped foot on the main dirt road that cut through the village. The tactical column split into two, with one half staying on the left side of the road and the other on the right. I happened to be on the right side with the intel officer and interpreter. We continued along the road until we approached the first building that had a makeshift sidewalk in front of it. At that point, we made our way onto the sidewalk and slowly began making our way to the middle of town. Glaring eyes stared us down the whole time. Little kids who had been playing soccer in the street paused to stare at us curiously. Some of the residents went inside their buildings and closed their doors.

I turned to the intel officer to get an idea of where he wanted to go. We were only a few hundred feet into the town, and it didn't seem as if many were willing to talk. He looked past me at a man who was selling things from a cart and seemed to be motioning for us to come toward him. I called for the interpreter to accompany us and then motioned for the rest of the scouts to kneel down and take cover. I then escorted the intel officer and interpreter to this mysterious man. As we got closer, I could see some type of fear and anxiety in his eyes. He appeared as if he wanted to tell us something, but we had to hurry. Through the interpreter, the officer began to ask relatively basic questions to make it seem as if the conversation was normal to any outside observers. The man spoke very quickly and in a hushed tone. He began answering the questions but then brushed them off and spoke quickly to the interpreter. The interpreter took it all in, nodded his head, and turned to us.

"We must leave now. He said that there is an ambush waiting for us down the road, and they will attack us if we continue down that way," the interpreter said.

The intel officer glanced down the road, turned to me, and told me we needed to move out and in a hurry. I glanced in the direction that the officer did, and I could see that the street was clearing out. I turned to my guys and told them we'd be heading back. Although I was disappointed that we wouldn't be going into the fight, the rational side of me knew that if an ambush did lie ahead, we would all probably get killed. Calmly, we all turned around and headed back the way we had come. As we left, the people who had gone into hiding came back out, and the nasty glares continued until we were out of sight.

About twenty minutes after we left, we arrived at the company outpost. I, along with several other scout leaders and the intel officer, debriefed our leadership, informing them of everything that had happened. When they were done with the scouts, we left to go back to our respective platoons, and they continued to talk with the intel officer. At the time, I wasn't too sure what else was discussed among the officers, but whatever it was must have had an impact because within a day, we were all headed back to the base.

When we returned to the base, it became very apparent that it wasn't to get some rest. Our brass was hovering over some maps and discussing things among themselves. Eventually, they called the platoon sergeants over to discuss some more events. In the meantime, we were all given some time to gather our thoughts, grab some chow, and get some snacks and cigarettes.

After a while, as I was sitting on my cot inside the hangar chatting with Sprenger, Lieutenant Snipes, Lieutenant May, and Staff Sergeant Phelps came over to my area and called the other Marines in our platoon over. Something seemed a bit off, but I couldn't put my finger on it. I'd just have to wait until Lieutenant Snipes and Staff Sergeant Phelps told us what was up.

Once everyone had gathered around, Lieutenant Snipes was the first to speak. He explained that since we were getting toward the end of our deployment, our company had to begin preparing for our trip back to the States. A few Marines were going to be sent as a forward party to begin ensuring everything stateside was ready for us. Our XO, Lieutenant Earlie Walker, was going to be heading back early to get everything prepared for us. As such, he needed to go back to Camp Baharia to get everything prepared there before he left. Once everyone got back to Baharia, he would take a few Marines with him back to the States.

That left the company executive officer position open, and it needed to be filled immediately. Captain Shepard decided that the position would best be held by Lieutenant Snipes. With Lieutenant Snipes leaving to be the XO, Lieutenant May of Weapons Platoon was assigned to be our platoon commander, and Gunnery Sergeant Zenoni would be the acting platoon commander for Weapons Platoon. Obviously, this was great news for Lieutenant Snipes as it was basically a promotion for him, but it left us with a platoon commander we knew well but had no experience with.

The other piece of news was that prior to the rest of us going back to Baharia, we had one more mission to complete. The village that we had gone into was apparently much more important than we initially realized. During his discussion with the local man from the street, the intel officer discovered that a high-value target (HVT) was holed up in a building in the village. Our mission was to go in with several other units, as well as an Iraqi army unit, capture the HVT, and get out of there as fast as possible.

Lieutenant Snipes excused himself, and Lieutenant May began to give us the plan. The Outlaws would head out to a location about three hundred yards from the village a few hours before dawn. At daybreak, we would quickly make our way into the city with a few Iraqi army units attached to us, set up a perimeter around the building that held the HVT, have the Iraqis nab him, and then head back to base. He instructed us to get some sleep because we would be heading out in just a few hours to get into position.

We headed back to our cots to get some quick shut-eye. I didn't sleep much, though. With everything going on, my mind was going in every direction. A new platoon commander, an HVT raid, and going home soon. So much information and so little time to process it. I tossed and turned, and I may have slept for a little under an hour before I was woken by the fire watch. I threw my camouflage blouse back on, put my boots on, and gathered up my gear. All around me, the other scouts were doing the same in silence.

I went around to the rest of my team to see if they were doing OK. Then we headed over to where our vehicles were staged in preparation for the mission. The rest of the Outlaws were doing the same. Lieutenant May and Staff Sergeant Phelps made their way to our position and immediately began to run us through our mission once more. When Lieutenant May was certain we all understood our duties, he had us mount our vehicles so we would be ready for the signal to go.

About twenty minutes of twiddling my thumbs later, word was passed down over the company communications that we were ready to head out. The engines roared to life, the drivers put their blackout lights on, and the scouts who were popped out of the scout hatches donned their night vision goggles. The line of LAVs began to slowly move.

It was about two hours before dawn, with barely a star in the sky. Our company slowly made its way to the rendezvous point. I glanced to the front and back, and it was truly a sight to behold. It was like seeing a giant, dangerously armed snake slithering its way toward its prey. It sent a chill up my spine.

Thirty minutes had passed when we finally arrived at our destination. We were about two or three hundred yards away from the outskirts of the village. At our location, towering about forty feet into the air, was this massive mound of dirt. It kind of reminded me of a castle archer tower. The top of the mound was flat, and it seemed as if walls were erected at the top to protect whoever was located there.

A countdown was given over the radio, and as it reached one, all the engines were shut off simultaneously, and there was utter silence. I'm pretty sure you could have heard a pin drop. Staff Sergeant Phelps dropped down inside the turret and began to give us a quick briefing of what we were going to do. As we had two hours before the raid began, all of the LAVs were set up in a defensive 360 perimeter around the mound. Since no one had gotten much sleep the night before, word was given to set up fire watch within each vehicle, with one LAV Marine and one scout per vehicle providing lookout for an hour while the others rested. Some of the vehicle commanders were deploying their scouts to provide perimeter security, and some just had their scouts stay inside the scout compartment.

Phelps decided he wanted the former. He had me take my team to the mound and set up a lookout post on top so we could provide overwatch for them. He told me to make sure everyone got some rest, though. So we opened the scout hatch and made our way to the top of the mound. Once there, I set up a schedule so there were two Marines awake and two resting at all times. I had the first shift along with Redd, so we both just sat there and kept an eye on the village. And we waited and waited for what seemed like an eternity. After a while, I glanced down at my watch and saw that our shift was over. We woke up Barajas and Zabala, and they took over our positions. I found a small spot on the ground, took off my helmet, used it as a headrest, and closed my eyes. I was out in seconds.

A half hour passed, and Barajas and Zabala woke Redd and me up. I wanted to make sure everyone was up and ready to go before the raid began, so I ensured that my shift was shortened. Redd and I got up and got in positions next to Zabala and Barajas. We kept an eye on the village and the surrounding area. From time to time, I would look down at our vehicle, which was about one hundred feet away, just to make sure everything was OK. I was slightly concerned that there was no one standing up in the turret, but I figured they had it all sorted out.

Dawn slowly crept up on us, and I watched the horizon as the sun began to make its way into the sky. Scouts from the other vehicles were beginning to make their way back to their LAVs, and drivers were making sure everything was good to go before the raid. I stared in the distance at our vehicle, and not a soul stirred. I was beginning to get nervous, but I didn't want to move my team back without Phelps giving us the word. And I was really pissed at myself that I hadn't brought our comm gear with us. So for about another five minutes, we sat there anxiously awaiting someone to pop up and tell us to make our way back. And then suddenly, the air was filled with the roar of engines. All around us, the scouts were mounting up into their vehicles, and engines were rumbling and ready to go. I looked back at our LAV and still saw no signs of life. Now I was getting really worried. My scouts were looking to me for an answer, and I had no idea what to say. I couldn't figure out why the hell no one from our vehicle was calling for us to mount up.

Frustrated, I decided to have us all make our way back to the vehicle. I told my team that we would quickly run back and find out what was going on. As we rose from our positions, though, the LAVs in our company began to move out one by one. Now I was really concerned. We were about to be stranded. At that time, I decided to forego safety and told my team to haul ass to our vehicle. No shot in hell was I going to be left alone in the middle of nowhere.

We were about twenty feet away from our vehicle when I finally saw Staff Sergeant Phelps rise from his turret. I could hear some other commotion inside as well. Bleary eyed, Phelps was screaming at us to mount up and yelling at Rankin to start the vehicle. By the time my team got into the vehicle and secured the doors, the rest of the company was out of sight. Sergeant Honigsberg popped out of his turret hatch and looked back at me. I glanced over and gave him a "What the fuck?" look. Knowing exactly what I wanted to say, he just shook his head and quickly looked at Phelps. Enough said.

Staff Sergeant Phelps gave Rankin the command to move out and catch up with the rest of the company. Rankin gunned the engine, the LAV kicked up dust, and we were hauling ass to get to our destination. It only took us about three or four minutes before the rest of the company came into view. All the vehicles were set up in their defensive positions in the middle of the town. Lieutenant May's vehicle, along with a pickup truck carrying some of the Iraqi army soldiers, was situated in the middle of the road outside of the building that was supposed to house the HVT. We pulled up alongside May's vehicle, and Phelps had me and the rest of the scouts jump out and provide close perimeter security around our vehicle. Lieutenant May looked over at Phelps and then down at me. He threw his hands up in the air in exasperation, and I quickly glanced over at Phelps. He knowingly nodded and then went back to concentrating on the mission.

One point of the mission was not to actually do the work ourselves. At this point during the war, there was a heavy push to stand up the Iraqi army and have them either do all of the work or at least assist them in completing the mission. In our case, we were there only for support. So when we pulled up, the Iraqi soldiers in the back of the pickup truck had already deployed and begun the raid in the house. In fact, since we were late, they had already been inside the house for a few minutes, so by the time we arrived, it was only a minute or two longer before they exited the house with the HVT in tow. They quickly threw him into the back of the truck and got in with him. Once they were all inside, Lieutenant May gave the order to move out. All the LAVs began leaving the town with the pickup carrying the HVT located in the center of the column.

All in all, the entire mission lasted no more than twenty minutes from beginning to end. The point wasn't to level the town. It was to get in and out with little to no confrontation. In that case, the mission was successful.

I could tell as we left the city and made our way back to the base that things were about to get heated. Lieutenant May had a look on his face that could kill, and Staff Sergeant Phelps seemed very nervous. I was definitely not looking forward to the debrief.

# CHAPTER 39
# LEADERSHIP

The trip back to the base was quiet. The usual internal radio banter was non-existent. When we got back, we quietly dismounted our vehicle, grabbed our gear, and headed to our cots in the hangar. Out of the corner of my eye, I could see several of the officers speaking to Staff Sergeant Phelps about what had happened. There was no yelling going on, but I could tell our leadership was pissed.

Honigsberg made his way over to my cot, and we started talking about what had gone down.

"Honnie," I said, calling him by his nickname, "what the hell happened? You guys left us hanging out there."

"Dude, it wasn't my fault, I swear," Honigsberg said. "Phelps didn't want Rankin pulling fire watch so he split it up between he and I. He had me do first watch and then he was taking second watch."

Honigsberg paused for a moment to make sure Phelps wasn't around and then continued, "After I finished my fire watch, I woke him up and then I fell asleep. Next thing I know, I wake up and I see Phelps passed out in the turret. And, on top of that, his fucking comm helmet was disconnected so he never heard a thing. I woke his ass up and I think that's when he realized he fucked up. He woke up Rankin, had you guys come back, and then we met up with Mays' vehicle."

"Dude, he's screwed," I said.

"Yeah, no shit. Glad it's not me," Honigsberg replied.

We continued to chat for a few more minutes before we were approached by Lieutenants Snipes and May. They seemed very concerned over the whole ordeal and began to question us. Honigsberg reiterated everything he had said to me, and then they both turned to me to get my side of the story. I rehashed what Honigsberg said and then added our part of the story from where my team and I were positioned. They both thanked us for giving them our side of the story and left.

A day later, we were all goofing around in the hangar, packing up our gear for the ride back to Camp Baharia the next morning. Sergeant Travis Madden headed over to where I was and we started talking for a bit. After a few minutes, Lieutenants May and Snipes headed over to where we were and called for the rest of the platoon to meet at their location. Once everyone was huddled around, Lieutenant May began to discuss what had happened during the raid. He stated that Phelps was going to be working for Lieutenant Walker as part of the advance party to go back home. As such, he was packing up his gear and heading back to Baharia in the next few hours. In his place, Sergeant Madden would be the acting platoon sergeant.

While it felt kind of weird having Phelps lose his position, I was thrilled to have Madden as our platoon sergeant. Madden, a tall, lanky, red-haired guy from Kansas, was a very smart, firm yet fair Marine whom everyone throughout the company had a lot of respect for. What made it even better was that I considered Madden a very good friend and had known him since I first entered the fleet, as he was also with me on my first deployment. I looked around and saw that I wasn't the only one excited about the change. The whole platoon had a slight grin on their faces. This was definitely going to be a good change of pace for everyone.

Once Lieutenant May was done discussing the change with us, he and Madden left to discuss other matters. I turned to Sprenger, and we both started talking about how great it was going to be with Madden in charge. We finished packing our gear and went about our business for the rest of the day.

Early the next morning as we were getting ready to leave on our trek back to Baharia, I realized it was going to be an even more enjoyable experience having Madden as the platoon sergeant. As he was replacing Phelps, he would also be my vehicle commander. I was totally psyched. Madden was good at rigging the comm gear so we could listen to music, so I knew we were going to have a nice ride back.

Just before dawn, our company parted ways with Iskandariyah. We were finally on our way back to Baharia. It felt as if a huge weight was being lifted off our shoulders. We were headed back to our home. And with only a month or so to go, our deployment was drawing down. There was finally a light at the end of the tunnel. As we'd soon learn, we still weren't clear, but at least there was hope. That ride back was one of the best and most enjoyable road marches I experienced in Iraq. Everything seemed perfect.

# CHAPTER 40
# THE MECHANIC

Upon our return to Baharia, things seemed to be looking up. In addition to the change of leadership in our platoon, we also had some shifting of vehicle crews. Due to the various events that had occurred in the past and the harsh environmental conditions in the desert taking a toll on our vehicles, our platoon was being broken apart to help shore up the other platoons. After all was said and done, our platoon was down to only three vehicles and three scout teams. Sergeant Learn, his crew, and scout team all moved over to Third Platoon. That left us with Sergeant Krall, Lieutenant May, and Sergeant Madden's crew.

For the first couple of days after we returned, none of the platoons were doing much more than maintaining the vehicles and our equipment. We'd make a few runs to the PX to restock our snacks and cigarettes, but the rest of the time, we were given free reign to do what we wanted within the camp walls. I spent most of my time either at the internet center sending emails and playing video games or back at the hooch playing cards or doing something else to occupy my time. Once patrols resumed, our platoon was mostly left out of it since we were one vehicle short. We did run odd missions here and there, but nothing of significance. This routine lasted for about three weeks, which brought us to the end of August and into early September.

At this point, excitement was in the air. We had been informed that Alpha Company, our replacements, was on their way from the States. Also, we had been informed that another assault on Fallujah was imminent. Insurgents had regrouped within the city and had resumed their assaults on American forces. This time around there was going to be no holding back; it would be a full-on assault.

It had been about three or four weeks since we had gotten back from Iskandariyah, and the boredom was really starting to set in. I was jealous of the other platoons because they were now doing patrols on a daily basis and were participating in the precursor to the second assault on Fallujah. Nearly every day, sitting inside the hooch on my cot, I could hear the familiar sound of an LAV firing rounds, the artillery units firing rounds from Camp Fallujah next door, or an IED going off in the distance. And, as we had grown accustomed to by this time, mortars and rockets landed in and around our base on a near-daily basis. The only benefit to staying on base the whole time was that I could visit the internet center as much as I wanted. But that's not why we were there, that wasn't our mission. And because of that, I grew bored extremely fast, as did the rest of the guys in the platoon.

Word was spreading that the Alpha Company Marines had finally arrived in Kuwait and were readying their vehicles for the road march to our base. One day in early September, Lieutenant May and Sergeant Madden had us all meet out by where our vehicles were staged. Klinger, Sprenger, Honigsberg, Nava, and I were all sitting around bullshitting about some kind of random stuff, so when the word was passed to us that we needed to meet outside, we slowly rose, grabbed our rifles, and made our way to where May and Madden were. We figured it was going to be another speech on being prepared, doing training to stay active, or some other random bit of news that was passed on a daily basis.

As we began walking over to where we were told, I noticed that Lieutenant Snipes was speaking with Lieutenant May. When everyone finally converged on the spot where Lieutenant May wanted us, he began to speak. In short, he informed us that Alpha Company was ready to move north and make their way to Camp Baharia. As had been the case with us, once they arrived at Camp Scania, they would need to be escorted to our location, not so much for protection but to ensure they wouldn't get lost. We found out in the time that we had been at Baharia that quite a few convoys that were trying to get to either Camp Baharia or Fallujah got lost due to misleading highway signs. In one case, a convoy misread a sign and headed directly into the center of the city of Fallujah rather than to Camp Fallujah. So to make sure that didn't happen again, Alpha Company was requesting that the Outlaws send an escort to lead them back to Camp Baharia.

Lieutenant May and Sergeant Madden broke out a map and laid out the plan of what routes we would be taking, what time we would be leaving, and when we expected to rendezvous with Alpha. It seemed very simple and low risk. We'd done several route patrols along some of the roads, so it was nothing out of the ordinary. The only thing that was lingering in the back of my head was that in two weeks we'd be headed back to

Kuwait, and I was concerned that at the last minute, someone else would get hurt, something that I was hoping would not happen to our company again. We had lost enough.

Lieutenant May then informed us why Lieutenant Snipes was in attendance. As we were down one vehicle, Lieutenant Snipes would be taking his crew and vehicle with us to plus up our numbers for the road march down.

After Lieutenant May finished giving his orders, we all headed back to our hooch, and there was excitement in the air. This was like the beginning of the end. We'd pick them up, get Alpha accustomed to the area, and then head home. Everyone quickly packed his gear to get ready for the patrol the next day. Tomorrow could not come soon enough.

I tossed and turned that night because I was so anxious. When morning came, I double checked all my gear, ran to the chow hall to get some grub, and then sat around until we were getting ready to go. Eventually, Sergeant Madden came into the hooch and informed us it was time. We all made our way to our vehicles and began loading our gear. This was going to be easy, so I didn't pack too much—just enough for a road trip plus some snacks and some music for the long trip.

Lieutenant May and Lieutenant Snipes walked out from the command center and made their way over to the vehicles. Before we got into our vehicles, Lieutenant May mentioned that he wanted to ensure that everyone got back safely, so he advised all the scouts to stand no more than chest level out of the scout hatches and for the vehicle crew to do the same. It was as if he had read my mind. No need to endanger the Marines so close to going home.

Lieutenant May gave the order to mount up and start the vehicles. The engines came to life, Lieutenant May ensured everyone was good to go, and then he gave the order to begin the long road march to Scania.

As we left the gates of Baharia, I made sure Redd and I were no more than chest high. I gave a nod to the gate guard as we passed by, and we were finally on our way to Scania. It was truly the beginning to the end of a long, long journey. With Lieutenant Snipes in the road march, we switched up the order of the vehicles we normally had for patrols. Sergeant Madden decided he wanted to be the lead vehicle heading toward Scania. Typically, the platoon sergeant's vehicle is the third vehicle, but Madden would have none of that for this trip. So we ended up being the point vehicle, with Sergeant Krall directly behind us, followed by Lieutenant Snipes's vehicle, and Lieutenant May's vehicle was rear security.

We made the left-hand turn onto the main route, gave each vehicle about two hundred feet of separation, and began our eight-hour trip to Scania. We could get there faster, but we had to travel in the vicinity of 40 mph unless otherwise told. I clicked on the internal comm in my helmet and called over to Sergeant Madden and Corporal Sprenger, wondering if they were going to throw the music on anytime soon. I needed something to occupy the time.

BBBBBOOOOOOOOOOOMMMMMMM!

A thunderous explosion rocked the vehicle. I looked around, frantically wondering if we had been hit and quickly concluded we hadn't. In the distance I could see Krall's vehicle was fine as well, but there was a lot of commotion coming from the back. Sergeant Madden jumped onto the internal radio really quick and told me

Krall's vehicle was hit; the vehicle was fine, but Herman was hit. Madden ordered us to stay in the vehicle. Krall's vehicle was going to quickly patch up Lance Corporal Herman, and we'd make a beeline for the battalion aid station (BAS) on Camp Fallujah, where he could get immediate attention.

No more than five minutes passed before we were speeding off to Camp Fallujah. They must have known we were coming because they quickly hurried us through the gate. We sped through the base and stopped right in front of the BAS. A few corpsmen were already waiting for us to arrive, so I watched as they quickly took Herman off of the vehicle and into the BAS with Lieutenant May and Lieutenant Snipes right behind him. In the meantime, I could see Shearer and Doc Barajas talking to some of the other corpsman and trying to clean the blood off of Shearer's vest. It was very apparent Shearer was both shocked and frustrated because he was getting annoyed with all the corpsman bothering him. He wanted them to attend to Herman and not worry about him.

Everything had happened so fast that I realized I hadn't had time to even think about what had unfolded. Prior to becoming a section leader, I was on the same vehicle as Herman. He was one of my scouts, and a damn good one at that. But he wasn't a scout by trade. He was the platoon's mechanic. Herman worked harder than all the other guys in our platoon because he had to do two jobs. When the rest of us were relaxing in the hooch or going to the chow hall, Herman was busting his ass fixing the vehicles. I came to rely on Herman too. He really knew his stuff, and I could always trust that he was watching my back. And the best thing about Herman was that regardless of the amount of crap he had to deal with, he would do what he was told. Sure, he would be pissed, but he would do it to the best of his ability. He was a damn fine Marine in my eyes.

The other thing that kept on going through my head was that had I not been promoted to section leader, it could have been me. All these different scenarios kept going through my head about how it could have or should have been me instead of Herman.

While Lieutenants May and Snipes were still in BAS, we were all trying to figure out exactly what had happened. And when we did figure it out, it was bizarre that Herman even got hit.

Apparently, as we were heading down the road, the triggerman for the IED pulled the trigger but far past the moment when he should have. The IED exploded when the whole platoon had already passed it by about one hundred yards. We figured that a piece of the shrapnel from the explosion must have somehow flown toward Krall's vehicle and hit Herman in the face. Fortunately for Herman, the piece of shrapnel grazed across his face rather than hit him full on which would have most likely killed him. It hit him on the side of the face, producing a gory wound that extended from his nose to the right ear.

When our platoon came to a halt after the explosion, Shearer, who had switched out positions with Herman for a portion of the ride, was calling from inside the vehicle to Herman to find out what happened. Herman was motionless. A few seconds later, Shearer saw blood come down Herman's uniform, and he immediately went into action. He opened the back scout hatch, sat Herman down on the bench inside the vehicle, broke out his first aid kit, and began patching up Herman's face as best he could. When Shearer ran out of gauze, Corporals Forsyth and Biorn began taking apart their kits and giving Shearer theirs. Doc Barajas showed up and began to apply more direct first aid. And during this whole time, rather than scream in pain, Herman, being the hard-ass he was, was cussing up a storm because he was pissed off that he got hit. It just reinforced my view of his strength of character.

After about twenty minutes or so, Lieutenants May and Snipes emerged from the BAS and made their way back to their vehicles. Lieutenant May threw on his gear and told Madden that we were still moving on toward Scania. Herman was being attended to and was in critical condition, but the corpsmen believed he would live and be all right.

Madden relayed the information to the rest of us as the vehicle was starting up. I was relieved to a point. I was really glad that Herman was not killed, but it was still painful knowing he was wounded. On our way out of the gates of Camp Fallujah, I was hoping for the best for him.

Fortunately, the rest of the trip down to Scania was uneventful. It just hurt knowing that we were one man short.

# CHAPTER 41
# ALPHA COMPANY

The mood of the platoon had changed from excited prior to leaving Baharia to downright disheartened when we arrived at Camp Scania. Picking up Alpha Company was supposed to be the beginning of the end. And that end was not supposed to include another one of our brothers hurt or dead. Thankfully, Herman was going to live to see another day, but it was still concerning knowing that he was severely injured.

When we finally arrived, word must have passed to Alpha Company that we had an incident on the way down there. We pulled into the gravel parking lot next to the LAVs from Alpha Company, dismounted, and walked over to where some of the Marines from Alpha were sitting around. In the mix I could see some familiar faces. Sergeant Martin Basso, a friend of mine from Infantry School, and Staff Sergeant Chris Keisler, one of my old platoon sergeants, came over and struck up conversation with a few of us asking what had happened. We rehashed the story, and they both expressed their condolences. I could tell they were both genuinely concerned for us as well as themselves. I'm sure the last thing they wanted to hear on their first day in country was that a fellow Marine was severely wounded. It's not exactly the best welcoming present.

After a few minutes of sitting around, we got word that we would be grabbing some chow before heading out. We all headed to the chow hall, grabbed some pretty decent food, and made our way to the long tables. I sought out Basso and sat down next to him. Sprenger and Klinger accompanied me and sat on either side of the table. Eventually, Staff Sergeant Keisler made his way over to our location and sat beside Basso. For the next half hour or so, we began to retell some of our experiences in Fallujah and answer as many questions as they had for us. We also asked them questions about any gossip they heard and how things were back home.

The chow hall began to fill up with a lot of Marines from other units, and it became apparent people were waiting on us to get up, so after devouring what was left on our trays, we stood up and headed back toward the vehicles. When we got back to where we had parked, we found out that we wouldn't be heading out for a few more hours because they wanted to complete this leg of the road march at night so as to reduce the possibility of getting hit by an IED. Since I was a bit tired from the ride down, I had a smoke, lay down on the ground next to my vehicle, and used my helmet as a headrest so I could catch a few zees.

A couple of hours passed by, and nightfall came. All the Marines began to wrap up what they were doing and started putting their gear on and mounting up into the vehicles. Lieutenant May, Lieutenant Snipes, and the officers from Alpha Company, along with the platoon sergeants, were gathered around in a circle going over the route back to Baharia one more time. They wanted to ensure no one got lost. After a few minutes of discussion, Lieutenant May, Lieutenant Snipes, and Sergeant Madden headed back to our vehicles and instructed everyone to get ready to move out. Once they were aboard their LAVs, they rogered up over the communications channel, and the engines roared to life. A couple minutes passed, and the road march back began.

The trip back to Baharia seemed to go by a bit quicker. It was probably due to the fact we were going a bit faster than when we headed down. And it also helped that there were no incidents on the way back. We pulled into Baharia shortly after dawn, and I was dead tired, as was pretty much everyone else. Thankfully, rather than have everyone gather to do a debrief, the officers dismissed us and told us to get some sleep. I immediately headed back to the hooch and passed out.

It was coming up on noon when I finally awoke from my nap. Some of the other guys from the platoon were already up, and word was spreading that there was going to be a company formation after lunch. I quickly threw on my clothes, grabbed Klinger and Sprenger, and headed over to the chow hall to get a bite to eat before formation.

After lunch, we headed back to our company area and saw some Marines already getting into formation. As everyone else started trickling back from chow, the formation grew bigger and bigger. Across from us, Alpha Company was also getting into formation. It took about twenty minutes or so before all the Marines from both companies were in formation.

One thing that stood out the most was the difference between the two companies. At this point, our company had been through hell and back. We had been mortared almost daily; had been in constant contact with IEDs and firefights; had slept roughly four to six hours a day; had shit, showered, and shaved when we could; had eaten when there was time; and had lost some good friends along the way. We had done and experienced all of this together, and because of that, we had become a close-knit family. Sure, there was still order and discipline among the ranks, but it came not out of fear or structure but instead out of respect, admiration, and camaraderie. We were what they called one salty group of Marines.

Opposite us stood a company that resembled what we had been six months prior: clean cammies, rigid bodies, perfectly maintained vehicles and weapons, and spotless gear. Captain Shepard emerged from the command center and began to address the two companies. As he spoke, mortars could be heard hitting just outside the walls of Baharia. A volley of artillery shells was then fired in return from Camp Fallujah. The thunderous booms from both could be heard in the distance. We had grown so accustomed to the noise that hardly any of us so much as flinched. On the other hand, quite a few Marines from Alpha flinched or made moves that looked as if they were ready to take cover in the bunkers. Nearly all of us gave a good chuckle at the situation, and I even saw Captain Shepard crack a grin. Soon enough, our fellow Marines from Alpha would be as familiar with the sounds as we were.

Captain Shepard informed us that Alpha Company would be taking over our operations. Over the next few days, we would be teaming up with our Alpha Company counterparts and conducting patrols with them to give them an idea of what we did on a daily basis.

We'd also go over lessons learned and other information we had gathered from the field. This was very similar to what had occurred when we first came to Baharia six months ago and did a left seat, right seat with the Army. In addition, we'd be readying our vehicles and gear for a trip back to Kuwait and, eventually, the United States.

Over the next few days prior to our departure to Kuwait, we began to conduct patrols with our counterparts from Alpha. It just so happened that Staff Sergeant Keisler and Sergeant Basso's platoon was being teamed up with us. Two vehicles from our platoon, typically Lieutenant May's vehicle and my vehicle, would accompany Staff Sergeant Keisler's vehicle and his platoon commander's vehicle on patrols in and around our area of operations. On these patrols, we would point out previous firefights, typical IED placements, and other information we thought would be useful to them as they began doing patrols. I found myself giving Basso pointers on how to protect himself and his scout team while standing up in the scout hatches as well as how to conduct foot patrols when they had to dismount.

When we weren't conducting patrols, we were packing up our stuff to take home. I packed all of my gear that I wouldn't need for the road march down to Kuwait. I also packed some other things I had acquired along the way—mementos, pictures, DVDs, and stuff like that. The things that I couldn't bring with me, I tried to sell to the Marines from Alpha. In fact, nearly everyone else in our company was doing the same thing. It seemed to be a time-honored tradition. The resident company would sell items to the incoming company, things like mattress pads for the cots, small refrigerators, games, etc. Refrigerators were actually one of the hottest commodities going, and I happened to be one of the few to own one. I ended up selling mine to Basso for seventy-five dollars, which was about half of what I bought it for when I got it from the PX. Many of the other guys ended up selling a lot of their stuff as well, so their load going home was lighter. It was like one giant yard sale.

The last day of our stay in Camp Baharia was, in a way, emotional. Baharia was a place that we had come to know as home. So many memories, both good and bad, had occurred at or around the base over the last seven months, and it was hard knowing that we'd leave it behind. We'd be heading home soon and it was great to know we'd be back with family and friends in the States, but Baharia was a place where permanent friendships were forged and memories were made. And most importantly, the friends and fellow Marines who had been lost had their names emblazoned on a memorial that was standing in the middle of camp. That memorial had become a symbol of the hardships our company had endured. To leave it behind was to say good-bye to dear friends.

On our last day, we staged all of our vehicles in one long line and began loading them up with our gear. Some of it we loaded onto the vehicles, and other things that couldn't fit in the vehicles, such as our sea bags, we loaded onto pallets that would be shipped down to Kuwait and then loaded onto the planes that would take us home. After I finished loading up my gear, I met up with a few of my friends from Alpha and wished them well on their stay. Once I was done making my rounds, I headed back to the vehicles to wait until we were ready to go. I passed time by talking to some of the other guys, playing a little hackey-sack, or just twiddling my thumbs.

When we got the call later on that day to mount up, I knew our time there was over. I grabbed my gear, donned my vest and helmet, slung my rifle over my shoulder, and jumped into the back of my vehicle for one last road march. Eventually, the line of LAVs began to slowly move toward the gates of Baharia like a caterpillar inching its way forward. As I passed the Outlaw memorial dedicated to our fallen brothers, I whispered one last good-bye and wished them eternal peace. That was the last time I looked back.

## CHAPTER 42
# HEADED BACK

Our trip back to Kuwait was not much to talk about. The only thing that comes to mind is that it was a very, very long drive. It did seem to go a bit faster than our trip up to Baharia, but it was still long. It wasn't until we arrived at the Kuwait border that I began to perk up a bit. The familiar barbed-wire fence was still there, separating destruction from paradise. It still came as a shock to me that just by crossing the border there was such a huge difference in surroundings. Gone was the constant reminder of war. All around us as we made our way through Kuwait were well-maintained BMWs and Mercedes driving past us at high speeds. Tall, glimmering buildings could be seen in the distance, surrounded by small cities. Even the sand in the desert seemed cleaner.

Before we could take off, we had to make a stop at Camp Arifjan, one of the largest US bases in Kuwait. Prior to the vehicles being shipped back to the United States, they needed to go through what is called a wash down. When vehicles go overseas, they go through extensive exercises or operations. Not only do they accrue a lot of dirt and sand, they can also harbor bacteria, bugs, or parasites that are foreign to US soil. To ensure we didn't bring back anything, we had to give the vehicles a very thorough cleaning. And it's not an ordinary cleaning either. I'm talking about "break out your toothbrush and scrub down the hubcap bolts" cleaning. For about three or four days, we would spend a good eight hours down at the wash ramp cleaning every nook and cranny of the vehicle and power washing the hell out of it. And just when we thought it was done, we'd call for an inspector to come over to check it out, and he'd find something else. It seemed like a never-ending process.

The only good thing was that when we weren't cleaning our vehicles, we were given permission to roam the base. Compared to the previous bases we had been to, this one was like Disney World. They had everything there: fast-food restaurants, a movie theater, a barbershop, a video game center, a telephone center, and so much more. We even had a small bus that our company was given to help transport everyone to and from the wash ramp. When I wasn't eating or playing video games, I would fight to drive the bus. I'd grab Madden, Sprenger, Klinger, or whoever had spare time and have them navigate while we zipped around exploring the base. I probably spent more time driving that bus than I did anything else during our stay at Arifjan. It wasn't that I loved to drive, it was that I hadn't driven in seven months, and the moment I was given the chance to do it, the joy of having that privilege was overwhelming. It truly was the small things in life that were making me happy.

A few days went by, and we finally passed our inspections. Our next stop was customs. A few Marines stayed behind with the vehicles as the rear party. The rest of us were shipped over to Camp Virginia along with our personal belongings and duffel bags to get inspected. When we got there, groups of us were ushered into tents and ordered to dump everything. These guys weren't looking for bugs and bacteria; they were looking for contraband. They wanted to go through everything to make sure we didn't bring back ammunition or weapons. So they had us go in groups of ten or so into a hooch. Inside, we had to take our cammies off to make sure we weren't hiding anything on our bodies, and then they dumped our gear and inspected everything. It took about fifteen minutes to go through all of our stuff, and when they were done, we had to neatly pack it all back up. It took the better part of a day to get the whole company through customs. No one really complained, though, because the next stop was the airport.

They piled all of us and our gear onto a bunch of buses and took us to Kuwait International Airport. Unlike our trip to Kuwait, we were treated like royalty and given an actual commercial airliner to fly home on. All of our gear was stowed away on the underside of the plane, and all we carried on board were any carry-on items we wanted and our rifles. The plane itself was huge in comparison to what I was accustomed to. The seats had plenty of legroom to stretch out, and the aisles seemed to be bigger than normal. While the plane was huge, it couldn't hold all of us at once, so we flew home in several planes. Not only were we flying home, but several other Marine Corps units were flying home as well. Fortunately, most of us were able to stick together and fly home on the same plane.

Prior to our departure, I heard someone in the back of the plane shout something about going home, and then everyone began to cheer. We had made it. Seven months had come and gone, and we were finally on our way home. The plane began to roll down the runway and then slowly started to lift into the nighttime sky. As the plane banked to the right, I looked toward the window to my right and saw the city lights below me. I looked forward, rested my chin on my chest, and closed my eyes.

So long, Iraq, it was nice knowing you. And good-bye, dear friends. You may not be with us anymore, but you will never be forgotten and will always be missed.

With that, I fell asleep.

# CHAPTER 43
# AFTERMATH

A "short" eighteen-hour flight later, the plane touched down safely in North Carolina. As the plane began to slow down and make its way off the runway, a bunch of shouts and cheers erupted from all of us. We were finally home. It felt so good to be home, it was almost unreal. Seven long, grueling months had finally come to an end.

We stepped out of the plane and onto the tarmac. Awaiting us were tons of family members who had made the trek to the airport to see their loved ones early. Wives and children ran and jumped into their husbands' and boyfriends' and fathers' outstretched arms. Tears streamed down dozens of faces. It was truly an emotional moment.

Our sea bags and gear were lined up on the tarmac. I knew my family was back at Lejeune waiting for me, so I quickly found my gear and made my way to the bus. It took a good amount of time for everyone to find his gear and load up, mainly because some guys were still chatting with family members. Once everyone was set, the buses began the short trip back to Camp Lejeune.

My first deployment, we were offloaded from the ship directly onto the beach, so there was no real trip back to the base. This time was a totally different experience. As we made our way through a few of the small towns on the route back home, hundreds of people lined the roads, flags waving and Welcome Home signs held high. Chills ran down my spine—the good kind. It was a surreal experience.

It took about forty-five minutes to get back to our battalion headquarters. Our bus pulled up in front of the building, and we began to offload. To the right of the building, a tent was set up. A crowd of family members and a few Marines were there with arms wide open. A few junior Marines began unloading our gear while we sought out our loved ones.

I stepped off the bus and spotted my parents and aunt and uncle in the crowd. My mom waved her hands high in the air. I quickly walked in their direction and met up with them halfway. Tears streamed down our faces as we all hugged. We sat down at a nearby bench for a little while and reminisced about various things. All around, Marines and their families were doing the same thing. It was such a wonderful moment.

After about thirty minutes, I began to seek out some of my fellow Marines. While walking through the crowd, I spotted some of the Marines who had been sent back home with serious wounds. Simms and Rhinehart were both making their way through the crowd greeting everyone. I walked up to them, shook hands, and gave them both a quick hug. It was so good to know that they were all right for the most part.

As the day wore on, the crowd began to thin out. We were given orders to take the rest of the day off and enjoy it with our families. I headed out with my parents to grab some food and talk some more. The first thing we did was head to a local steakhouse, and I ordered a big, fat, juicy steak.

*****

A few days later, most of us left the base for a couple of weeks to get some much-needed vacation time. When everyone finally came back from leave about a month later, things began to change significantly. A good number of the Marines who wanted to deploy with the company had to extend their contracts in order to go. Because of this, many Marines began the process of checking out and eventually returning to civilian life when we got back. Others went on to new duty stations or were reassigned to other units in the battalion. Only a handful stuck with Delta Company, either to ride out their contracts or redeploy with the next Marine Expeditionary Unit (MEU). I was one of the former.

I still had about six months left on my contract, so I stuck around for a bit before moving to Headquarters Company for a short stint and then coming back to the Delta Company for the last couple of months. During that time, I was a witness to the changes that began to occur within the Outlaws. The atmosphere within the company was becoming noticeably different. For seven months, we had endured everything together: we had laughed together, we had cried together, and we had fought together. We had relied on one another to have our backs and would have given our lives to protect the others. We had built a relationship that was stronger than just rank:

we were a family, a brotherhood, sewn together by trust, respect, blood, tears, and sweat. Everything we had built together was slowly being torn apart.

The glue that had brought us all together, officers such as Lieutenant Snipes, Lieutenant Nunnally, and Lieutenant Rowell, as well as senior staff NCOs such as First Sergeant Sprague and Gunny Rossignol, started going their own ways. New officers and senior staff NCOs came in to replace them, and while they had respect for our accomplishments, these weren't the same men who would have taken their shirts off their back for us. They hadn't gone through the same events we did. Along with the senior staff, the rest of the company, the backbone of the Outlaws, began to go their own ways. Many left the service to take on new challenges in the civilian world, like Sprenger and Nava, and others went on to other units or duty stations. By December, only a couple months after we had returned home, the Delta Company I had come to know and love was completely different.

As I watched everyone go, I tried to cling to any aspect of my family that was left. I started forming stronger friendships with some of the Marines who stuck around. Simms, badly burned from head to toe, and I began to grow close. He was fighting to stay in the Corps but had to prove that he was capable of passing a physical fitness test. So every day for a few months, we would both go out to the pull-up bars, and I would assist him in doing as many as he could. He started off at zero, and over the months made his way up to doing a few unassisted. He would eventually stay with the Marine Corps for a few more years. It was friendships like this that kept me going and reminded me of the family we once had and the sacrifices so many had made.

Six months passed, and I made the decision to leave the Marine Corps and enter the civilian world. On my last day, I finished going through the checkout process and made my way over to the company office for my final farewell.

"Tanner, you sure you don't want to re-enlist?" Captain Quinlan asked, already knowing the answer.

"Sir, I really appreciate the offer, but I think it's time for me to start a new chapter in my life," I responded, feeling a slight tinge of guilt for leaving so much behind.

"All right, then, head out to formation so we can give you a proper send-off."

I walked outside and took my place.

"Company! Atten-hut!" a gruff voice yelled.

A half hour later, approaching the gate to leave, I glanced over at the passenger seat where I had placed the book Captain Quinlan had given me. What am I supposed to do with this thing? I wondered. A book of stories seemed like an odd parting gift. I thought about Captain Quinlan's final words again, the ones regarding writing something about my fellow Outlaws. At the time, it seemed like such an unusual request, but as time wore on and I approached the gates of Camp Lejeune, memories continued to flood my head, and I couldn't stop thinking about the family I was leaving behind. As I passed through the gates, I realized that I did have a story to tell.

# ACKNOWLEDGMENTS

After I left the Marine Corps and entered the civilian world, I started thinking more seriously about the story I could tell. The Outlaws had experienced so much, bringing us close and forming a bond that is stronger than family. Whether it was playing pranks on one another, having one another's back in combat, or being a shoulder to lean on when times got rough, these events made us form friendships that will last a lifetime.

The only thing missing was someone whom I felt would be able to relate to my experiences. It wasn't until a few individuals encouraged me to tell our story that I began to feel some of the anxiety and stress dissipate. Not only did these people give me the confidence I needed to tell our story, but when times were tough and I didn't have it in me to continue to write, they pushed me and gave me the support I needed to finish the task.

My wife, Melissa, has been my biggest cheerleader since I started writing in 2006. She's been my shoulder to lean on throughout this whole project. Without her unfaltering love and support, I truly believe I never would have been able to finish writing this book. I am so glad to have met and married such a wonderful and kind woman.

My two little boys, Joshua and Gavin, have given me so much during this time. Their youthful joy and happiness inspired me to continue writing when times were tough. They may not be able to read or understand this book now, but I hope when they do, it gives them a deep understanding and appreciation of the sacrifices our service members make on a daily basis.

If it weren't for my parents making me write essays for hours on end when I was in middle school, I never would have done my fellow Outlaws justice with this book. Their constant encouragement and dedication to ensure I was able to write well made the story of the Outlaws become a part of written history.

I cannot thank my fellow Outlaws enough for the support they provided me throughout this whole ordeal. Some memories were beginning to fade and some needed clarification, and I always knew I could rely on my brothers to help me out when I needed it most. I personally want to thank Brian Callendar, Daniel Botty, Justin Hall, Tyler Valks, Earlie Walker, Kevin Knox Nunnally, Irving Afraidofbear, Joshua Shearer, Alfonso Nava, Jason Sprenger, Michael Sprague, Larry Rossignol, Christopher Toms, Jeremiah Doub, Tony Russell, Jason Klinger, Jared Hendrickson, Brett Durbin, Jake Rhinehart, Jason Simms, Nicholas Santiago, Ryan Redd, Christopher Amstutz, and David Grove for reading each chapter as I wrote it and providing input along the way. Without your help, I wouldn't have done the Outlaws justice.

Finally, to all my fellow Outlaws, my time in the Marine Corps may have been short, but I can honestly say that to this day, I have never served with a finer group of men. It is a pleasure to have known you all, and it is an honor to call you my brothers.

Semper Fi.

# DELTA COMPANY OUTLAWS ROSTER

*February – September 2004*

# Headquarters Platoon

Captain Ladd W. Shepard
1st Lt. Earlie H. Walker
1st Sgt. Michael E. Sprague
Gunnery Sergeant Larry S. Rossignol

Gunnery Sergeant Roger A. Riggs
Sgt. John P. Flaherty
Sgt. Jamie C. Corcoran
Sgt. Richard A. Jibson
Sgt. Jake Rhinehart
Cpl. Cometa Amnath
Cpl. Joseph K. Clarkson
Cpl. Michael J. Campbell
Cpl. Christopher Z. Cubstead
Cpl. Stanley A. Roberts
Cpl. Tyler R. Valks
Cpl. Jermaine J. Whitley
Cpl. Gustavo G. Canas
Cpl. Mark A. Gauthier
Cpl. Matthew R. Johnston
Cpl. Raymond C. Jobe
Cpl. Randall D. Hansen
Cpl. Joseph L. Todd
LCpl. Amin Valdes
LCpl. David A. Ledbetter

LCpl. Michael Korutz
LCpl. Justin E. Englehart
LCpl. Vincent J. Anderson
LCpl. Robert D. Frazier
LCpl. Christopher S. Markus
LCpl. Michael E. Jelley
LCpl. Wesley A. Hatfield
LCpl. Eric D. Yarger
LCpl. Ray J. Parra
LCpl. James C. Fleischmann
LCpl. Thomas W. Furst
PFC Cesar R. Alvarado
HM2 Robert S. Hamilton

# First Platoon

1<sup>st</sup>Lt. David P. Snipes
SSgt. Randy J. Phelps

Sgt. Michael I. Honigsberg
Sgt. Gaw S. Jones Jr.
Sgt. Michael P. Krall
Sgt. Richard R. Learn
Sgt. Alfonso L. Nava
Cpl. Mark D. Biorn
Cpl. Miguel J. Forsyth
Cpl. Todd J. Herman
Cpl. Jason D. Klinger
Cpl. Cuba-Rodriguez
Cpl. Jason R. Sprenger
Cpl. Robert M. Tanner
LCpl. Jorge A. Duarte
LCpl. Francesca A. Fillicetti
LCpl. Adam B. Godsey
LCpl. Samuel L. Herzberg
LCpl. John R. Martuszewski Jr.
LCpl. Gilbert G. Pascua
LCpl. Peter A. Rankin
LCpl. Douglas M. Raymer
LCpl. Ryan A. Redd
LCpl. Joshua C. Shearer

LCpl. Louis T. Thorton
LCpl. Tyler L. Tracy
LCpl. Luis A. Zabala
HA Kristopher Barajas

# Second Platoon

1ˢᵗLt. Kevin K. Nunnally
SSgt. Michael K. Woods

Sgt. Travis D. Madden
Sgt. Marcus L. Rowe
Sgt. Alejandro J. Miller
Sgt. Nicholas Santiago
Cpl. Jon M. Angus
Cpl. Garett D. Bunkleman
Cpl. Jeffrey D. Lawrence
Cpl. Octaviano Mendoza
Cpl. Boris D. Swims
LCpl. Rodney A. Backues
LCpl. Jeffery J. Bertch
LCpl. Jeremiah M. Doub
LCpl. Scott E. Dougherty
LCpl. Ezekiel J. Drawhorn
LCpl. Brett J. Durbin
LCpl. Mark E. Engel
LCpl. Jason R. Gonzalez
LCpl. Jose G. Herrera
LCpl. Justin T. Hunt
LCpl. Epifanio F. Krause
LCpl. Richard Ryan
LCpl. Jerod L. Thompson

LCpl. Gabriel Wakonabo
PFC Nicholas A. Dobrowsky
PFC Joshua R. Woodard
PFC Rodricka A. Youmans
HN Adrian U. Weldon

# Third Platoon

1<sup>st</sup>Lt. Ronny T. Rowell
SSgt. Ronald Ducharme
SSgt. Ray B. Urquieta

Sgt. Jared A. Hendrickson
Sgt. Brian Callendar
Sgt. John D. Leuba
Cpl. Christopher P. Amstutz
Cpl. Daniel P. Botty
Cpl. Justin L. Hall
Cpl. Scott M. Vincent
Cpl. Joshua S. Wilfong
LCpl. Irving J. Afraidofbear Jr.
LCpl. Ronald M. Banasiak
LCpl. Timothy R. Creager
LCpl. Ryan D. Daugherty
LCpl. James Doscher
LCpl. James A. Haffa
LCpl. Jonathan C. Snyder
LCpl. Aric L. Spenard
LCpl. Bradley A. Swenson
LCpl. Jason P. Thiel
LCpl. Kenneth Torok
LCpl. Paul R. Valliere
LCpl. Patrick J. Walsh

LCpl. Jason R. Wheeler
LCpl. Russell H. Zinke
PFC Randy L. Williamson
PFC Christopher A. Wood
HM3 Aaron L. Ferguson

---
# **Weapons Platoon**
---

2[nd]Lt. Robert F. May
Gunnery Sergeant Dean D. Zenoni

Sgt. Troy L. Bradley
Sgt. Brian S. Burke
Sgt. Thomas J. Korabik
Cpl. Andre J. Alfaro
Cpl. Phillip A. Gregg
Cpl. Joseph W. Lorek
Cpl. Nicholas A. Mims
Cpl Tony M. Russell
Cpl. Jeremy W. Sansbury
Cpl. Jason Simms
Cpl. Terry L. Steele
Cpl. Marcus J. Untalan
Cpl. Joseph C. Weeks
LCpl. Keith A. Bridges
LCpl. Jason F. Delfeld
LCpl. Jacob I. Duran
LCpl. Luis A. Duran
LCpl. Trevor A. Hammett
LCpl. Stephen M. Hewitt
LCpl. John T. Leavelle Jr.
LCpl. Joseph A. Lyons
LCpl. Christopher L. Toms

PFC Leo A. Boren
PFC Patrick D. Elswick
PFC Daniel R. Fox
PFC Andrew J. Manzi
PFC Eric A. Wilk
HM3 Scott H. Appleby

# ABOUT THE AUTHOR

Robert M. Tanner is a former infantryman in the United States Marine Corps. During his time in the military, he was assigned to the Delta Company Outlaws, Second Light Armored Reconnaissance Battalion, Second Marine Division. Tanner's travels have taken him from the Mediterranean and Kosovo to Djibouti, the United Arab Emirates, and Fallujah. Following an honorable discharge from the Marines, he went on to complete his bachelor's in business management from Rowan University, his MBA from Georgian Court University, and finally, another bachelor's in web design and development from Full Sail University. He began his civilian career as a contract specialist for the United States Army and has worked his way through various positions to finally end up as a business systems analyst with the Department of Veterans Affairs. Tanner is happily married to his wife, Melissa, and they are the proud parents of two little boys, Joshua and Gavin.

To find out more about Robert Tanner and his time as a member of the Delta Company Outlaws or to contact him directly, visit www.memoirsofanoutlaw.com.

CPSIA information can be obtained at www.ICGtesting.com
Printed in the USA
LVOW132233270513

335680LV00001B/25/P